Cary L. Cooper, Ph.D., is Professor of Management Educational Methods in the Department of Management Sciences at the University of Manchester, Institute of Science and Technology, England. Dr. Cooper is the only American to hold a Chair in a British University in the field of management and organization behavior. He is also Editor-in-Chief of the international scholarly journal, *The Journal of Occupational Behavior.* In addition he has written 19 books and over 125 academic articles concerning the topics of job stress, developing social processes, and management skills.

Prentice-Hall, Inc., Englewood Cliffs, N.J. 07632 A SPECTRUM BOOK

THE
STRESS CHECK

coping with the stresses of life and work

Cary L. Cooper

University of Manchester
Institute of Science and Technology

Library of Congress Cataloging in Publication Data

Cooper, Cary L.
    The stress check.

    (A Spectrum Book)
    Bibliography: p.
    Includes index.
    1. Stress (Psychology) 2. Personality.
3. Family. 4. Work—Psychological aspects. I. Title.
BF575.S75C65   158   80-20796
ISBN 0-13-852640-0
ISBN 0-13-852632-X (pbk.)

Editorial/production supervision and interior design by Fred Bernardi
Cover design by Ira Shapiro
Manufacturing buyer: Cathie Lenard

A SPECTRUM BOOK

Printed in the United States of America

10 9 8 7 6 5 4 3 2 1

Prentice-Hall International, Inc., *London*
Prentice-Hall of Australia Pty. Limited, *Sydney*
Prentice-Hall of Canada, Ltd., *Toronto*
Prentice-Hall of India Private Limited, *New Delhi*
Prentice-Hall of Japan, Inc., *Tokyo*
Prentice-Hall of Southeast Asia Pte. Ltd., *Singapore*
Whitehall Books Limited, *Wellington, New Zealand*

*I should like to dedicate this book to
the following Coopers, my social support team:
June, Scott, Beth, Lillian, Harry, and Tabi.*

Contents

Preface

Stress in everyday life is greater than it has ever been. One doesn't have to be convinced of this reality by the media coverage of the death of an internationally known celebrity like Peter Sellers; the figures for coronary heart disease, alcoholism, and mental illness speak for themselves. They speak of human waste, of unfulfilled dreams, of shattered and disillusioned children, or as Ernest van den Haag so aptly put it, "of happiness and of despair we have no measure." The purpose of this book is to make individuals and organizations aware of the sources of stress at work and in life generally, how they may contribute to them, and what can be done to help the individual, his family, and the people he works with.

Although there is some truth to Dostoyevsky's view (in his book *Notes from Underground*) that "the whole work of man really seems to consist in nothing but proving to himself every minute that he is a man and not a piano-key," life at home and at work can be made more liveable and we can do something about it. We owe it not only to ourselves but also to the people who depend on us to create modes of living that facilitate well-being.

Similarly, the organizations we all work for should be responsible for humane work environments. They must consider their structures and policies in light of the needs and aspirations of the people who work for them. Organizations and the people who run them must face up to the reality of what James Baldwin wrote a number of years ago in a popular magazine: "It is a terrible, an inexorable, law that one cannot deny the humanity of another without diminishing one's own: in the face of one's victim, one sees oneself."

And finally, I have found working in the field of stress both satisfying and rewarding, and would like to thank my friend and colleague, Judi Marshall, for her encouragement, support, and help.

Cary L. Cooper

STRESS AND
ITS CONSEQUENCES
FOR HEALTH
AND WELL-BEING
part I

The Nature of Stress
chapter 1

Introduction

Work and life stress are currently topical issues among the ordinary public, educationalists, the "helping professions," occupational health medics, and others responsible for the well-being of people. We have been shocked by *Future Shock* (Toffler), aggravated by *A Types* (Friedman and Rosenman), transported by Transcendental Meditation, bemused by bio-rhythms, hysterically satiated by Reggie Perrin's desserts, and amused (yet horrified) by Joseph Heller's comment that *Something Happened*. But has anything *happened*? Have governments, health authorities, work organizations, or indeed individuals themselves, really committed themselves to systematic and continuous action plans designed to minimize unnecessary life and work stress, to substantially enhance the well-being of themselves or the people they are responsible for, or to confront the problems generated by societal changes likely to increase the pressures at work and in the home (e.g., dual-career family) over the next decade? The resounding answer must unfortunately be *no*. Only a handful of concerned people and organizations have even begun to seriously consider these issues. The time has long passed to simply hold another stress symposium, conference, or workshop; what we now need are well thought out preventive programs of stress management whose primary objective is to provide more liveable environments in the home and at work.

Many of my colleagues throughout the United States and Europe, who are keen to help facilitate substantive interventions to improve the quality of life generally, have found obstacles at all levels. We have found, for example, in the context of work stress, that company policy, management attitudes, and trade union behavior are the primary culprits, not by design but by inaction or lack of foresight—by ignoring the potential health hazards of many stressors at work, they are indirectly supporting the rising level of stress-related illnesses in industry. In England and Wales, for instance, the death rate from coronary heart disease in men between the ages of 35 to 44 nearly doubled between 1950 and 1973. (The same sort of increase applies to nearly all other developed countries in the West.) Indeed, 41 percent of all deaths in the 25- to 44-year old age group were due to cardiovascular disease. It is up to those of us working in and with industry to begin to effectively deal with these appalling statistics. The personnel specialist, for example, has a critical role to play here (in a work context), given his/her implicit responsibility for the well-being of an organization's employees. This will not be an easy task in a time of industrial stagnation; it will demand a high degree of risk-taking and courage, but the payoffs are potentially limitless. If we can make our industrial and public sector organizations more humane and caring, more people might want to work *for* and *with,* as opposed to *against,* them. As Wright (1975) has suggested: "Responsibility for maintaining health should be a reflection of the basic relationship between the individual and the organization for which he works."

In addition to "what others can do" for the individual at work and in the home, it is essential that each and every person who experiences the excessive pressures of life begins to help himself. Organizations and institutions can lay the foundation stones for better health and well-being, but it is up to the individual to reduce his/her own internal pressures or to redesign his/her own lifestyle to help him/herself. Unless the individual takes an active part in the process of stress prevention and coping, institutional or governmental policy changes will be of little use.

The purpose of this book, therefore, is twofold: (1) to provide the reader with some insight into the sources and effects of various life and work stressors, and (2) to make a small beginning in suggesting some alternative strategies or courses of action to help alleviate, minimize, or cope with them. In terms of the first objective, it is hoped we can help the reader to become more aware of and to locate the sources of his/her work, life, or personal stress. My second objective is not meant to be all embracing, that is, to provide "the answers" to various stress-related problems, but rather to begin the process of making one aware of a variety of techniques or action plans that the reader may not have considered before.

The book is divided into nine chapters. The first three chapters examine, respectively: the nature of stress; its effects on the individual, organization, and community; and its costs to society. The next three chapters focus on strategies of coping with personal stress in life; managing your Type A coronary-prone behavior; seeking social support; and reprogramming your lifestyle. Chapter 7 extends the personal stress approach a bit further by exploring the problems of contemporary marriage, particularly the future effects of dual-career marriages and increasing family mobility. And finally, the last two chapters explore the individual and organizational approaches to relieving stress at work, that is, what the organization can do to alleviate stress and what the individual can do to help him/herself at work.

Different Approaches to Understanding Stress

Stress (a word derived from Latin) was used popularly in the seventeenth century to mean *hardship, straits, adversity,* or *affliction.* During the late eighteenth century its use evolved to denote *force, pressure, strain,* or *strong effort,* with reference primarily to a person or to a person's organs or mental powers (Hinkle, 1973).

The idea that stress contributes to long-term ill health (rather than merely short-term discomfort implicit in the above definition) can also be found early on in the concept's development. In 1910, for example, Sir William Osler noted that angina pectoris was especially common among the Jewish members of the business community and he attributed this, in part, to their hectic pace of life: "Living an intense life, absorbed in his work, devoted to his pleasures, passionately devoted to his home, the nervous energy of the Jew is taxed to the uttermost, and his system is subjected to that stress and strain which seems to be a basic factor in so many cases of angina pectoris" (Osler, 1910).

Hans Selye (1946) was one of the first to try to explain the process of stress-related illness with his "general adaptation syndrome" theory. In it he described three stages an individual encounters in stressful situations:

1. the *alarm reaction* in which an initial shock phase of lowered resistance is followed by countershock during which the individual's defense mechanisms become active;

2. *resistance,* the stage of maximum adaptation and, hopefully, successful return to equilibrium for the individual. If, however, the stressor

continues or the defense does not work, he will move on to the third stage;

3. *exhaustion,* when adaptive mechanisms collapse.

This theory reflected the prevalent feeling of the thirties and forties, that stress could be understood exclusively by a simple stimulus-response model, as illustrated in Figure 1.1. Although many of the current definitions of stress still stick fairly closely to the stimulus-response or energy-exchange model of stress, there is a movement toward viewing it more as an *interactive process.*

Caplan (1964), adopting a simple stimulus-response approach, depicts man as reacting to situations with learned coping mechanisms activated by homeostatic principles and fueled by energies which are in finite supply. Problems arise when the organism's supplies are insufficient to meet the physical, psychological, and/or sociocultural demands made of them. Cofer and Appley (1964) offer a similar definition: "Stress is

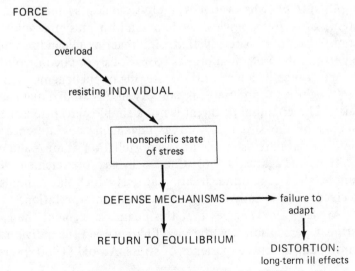

FIGURE 1.1   Stimulus-Response Model of Stress

the state of an organism where he perceived that his well-being (or integrity) is endangered and that he must divert all his energies to its protection." Basowitz, Persky, Korchin, and Grinker (1955) also bring out implications of overload: "We should not consider stress as imposed upon the organism, but as its response to internal or external processes which reach those threshold levels that strain its physical and psychological integrative capacities close to or beyond their limits," at the same time mentioning the response the individual makes as a necessary component of stress definition.

This more sophisticated viewpoint is particularly well articulated by Lazarus (1971) and is the beginning of interactionist thinking. While pointing out that both the environmental stimulus and the reacting individual are vital elements (one cannot refer to a stimulus as such unless it is part of a reactive situation), Lazarus (1971) emphasizes that it is the nature of the relationship between the two which is crucial: "Stress refers, then, to a very broad class of problems differentiated from other problem areas because it deals with *any demands which tax the system,* whatever it is, a physiological system, a social system, or a psychological system, and the response of that system." He goes on to say that the "reaction depends on how the person interprets or appraises (consciously or unconsciously) the significance of a harmful, threatening or challenging event."

"Cognitive appraisal" is an essentially individual-based affair: "The appraisal of threat is not a simple perception of the elements of the situation, but a judgement, an inference in which the data are assembled to a constellation of ideas and expectations" (Lazarus, 1966). Change in any one element, for example, the background situation against which the stimulus is perceived, can radically alter the perceiver's interpretation.

Appley (1962) agrees that this cognitive element (he calls it "threat perception") is the vital link between the individual's environment and his experience of stress. Arnold (1960) prefers the term "sense judgement" and emphasizes that elaborate levels of awareness are not necessarily involved.

Once this "perceptual viewpoint" becomes theoretically acceptable, we find that stress researchers soon seek to ascribe some of the (indisputable) individual variations in nature and levels of stress to characteristics of the individual, rather than, as before, concentrating mainly on the environment. Appley and Trumbull (1967) talk of a person's "vulnerability profile"— personality, demographic factors, physical makeup, past experience, and motivation will be the main considerations here—and provide substantiating research which found that "well-adjusted, integrated, mature" individuals showed less performance decrement in stress situations than did persons not so classified. They add that the more the stimulus relies on prior conditioning, the more individual differences are likely to play a part.

A term which we must clarify before proceeding is "load," that is, the environmental demand experienced by the individual. As we have seen, most writers focus on overload of the organism's capabilities as causing stress; engineering's use of the word encourages this interpretation. We now have, however, experimental evidence (e.g., studies of sensory isolation, stimulus impoverishment and social isolation) to show that underload too is "unacceptable." Kahn (1970) points to the implication from engineering that conditions of zero stress favor maximum life for the structure concerned and suggests that it is totally invalid to apply this to living organisms. Weick (1970), developing this idea, feels that a "more realistic view is that a person experiences more or less stress, not presence or absence of stress."

Drawing together the preceding two points, we see that rather than being either response- or situation-based, the concept of stress truly makes sense only when seen as imbalance in the context of an individual-environment transaction. Most writers endorse this person-environment fit model in their discussions, if not their definitions, of stress. This is summarized in Figure 1.2.

Cause and Effect of Stress

The implication that the effects of stress are somehow "undesirable" has been made several times above. While it is accepted by researchers that "stress" can have both short- and long-term adverse effects on an individual's mental and physical health, there is much debate as to the nature and probabilities of the causal relationships involved. We do not propose to become too entangled in the complexities of this material here (especially since much of it can only be assessed from a medical background).

The mental ill-effects of stress (e.g., anxiety, lowered self-

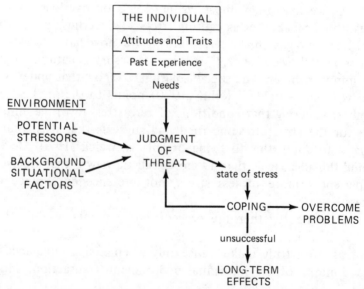

FIGURE 1.2   The Person-Environment Model of Stress

esteem, depression) are intuitively credible and are frequently used as measures of stress. Rather than being "effects by proof" they are very much "effects by definition." Over the last ten to fifteen years, stress has also been linked with various physical symptoms such as high blood pressure and blood cholesterol levels, rashes, and alopecia. These are physical signs of high activation levels and thus are also symptoms that the individual is "in a state of stress." Over time, these physical symptoms can have their own undesirable consequences; most notably, coronary heart disease, but also peptic ulcers, rheumatoid arthritis, and diabetes. This is how Hinkle (1973) summarizes the evidence on this topic:

> In other words, it might be said that, in man and in the higher animals, reactions to the environment which are mediated by the sense organs and the central nervous system have the capacity to influence any process within the organism that can be influenced by the gross motor behaviour of the organism itself, or by the alteration of any function of either the organism or of its component parts, which can be influenced by the skeletal or autonomic nervous system, or by the glands of internal secretion, acting alone or together. . . . Thus the potential magnitude of the effects . . . appears to be as great as the effects which can be produced by any other influences upon these processes, not even excluding those which destroy or permanently damage the systems that are involved in them.

While the general paradigm is constantly being supported by new evidence, the progression from stress experience to coronary heart disease is by no means 100 percent proven. Many other variables—such as personality, lifestyle, social support, occupation, diet, and cigarette smoking—have been identified as influencing the interactions involved. An adaptation of Carruthers' (1976) model, shown in Figure 1.3, (which was originally used with air traffic controllers) illustrates the complex factors involved. Underlying many writers' descriptions of this fatal

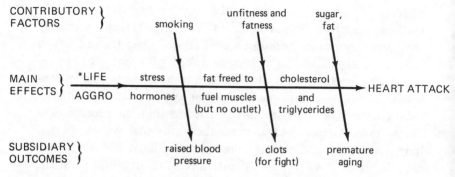

*LIFE AGGRO — refers to life 'aggravation'; stressors at work, in the home, etc.

FIGURE 1.3   Flight Path to a Heart Attack

sequence of effects is the belief that man reacts physically in threat situations, where physical discharge is no longer appropriate. The resulting "bottling up" only feeds his inner tension and over time has irreversible physiological consequences. The implications, too, that "stress" is the Black Plague of the twentieth century cannot be ignored.

Stress is acknowledged as a study topic of vital importance not only because of the mental and physical suffering it can cause individuals, but also because it may well make a substantial, if indirect, contribution to the social and economic problems of today's society. Many writers justify their interest in stress as a research topic by its cost to the national economy (Felton and Cole, 1963; Aldridge, 1970; Gillespie, 1974; Taylor, 1974). While the exact figures will not be quoted here, it is obvious that the economic cost of stress in terms of absenteeism, sick leave pay, and hospital bills is considerable.

Early Recognition of Stress Symptoms

At the behavioral level, and in a somewhat restricted context, several writers (mostly of the anecdotal general practitioner or company doctor type) have identified symptoms by which stress can be recognized (Kenton, 1974; Pettigrew, 1972; McGhee, 1963; Webber, 1966). Consistently mentioned are:

a. difficulty in thinking rationally and seeing all aspects of a problem
b. rigidity of views, prejudice
c. out-of-place aggression and irritability
d. withdrawal from relationships
e. excessive smoking
f. an inability to relax resulting in excessive drinking or a need for sleeping pills

To conclude, while the complexity and conditional nature of interactions between the individual and his environment make nonsense of any attempt to summarize life in a few simple, causal, one-to-one relationships, there is wide agreement, especially amongst the medical profession, that there is a strong link between experience of stress and "premature" death.

The Individual, Work, and Family Sources of Stress
chapter 2

Having examined the various definitions of stress and its historical nature as a concept, it is important to briefly identify some of the sources of life stress. There are three primary precursors: the personality of the individual concerned, his/her work environment, and the family. By examining each of these, we hope to draw attention to the main aspects of stress in people's lives and, therefore, to provide the reader later in the book with various strategies for dealing with them.

THE STRESSFUL PERSON

Sources of pressure in life evoke different reactions from different people. Some people are better able to cope with these stressors than others; they adapt their behavior in a way that meets the environmental challenge. On the other hand, some people are more characterologically predisposed to stress, that is, they are unable to cope or adapt to the stress-provoking situation. Many factors may contribute to these differences— personality, motivation, being well- or ill-equipped to deal with problems in a particular area of expertise, fluctuations in abilities (particularly with age), insight into one's own motivations and weaknesses, etc. It is necessary to look, therefore, at those characteristics of the individual that are predisposers to stress. Most of the research in this area has been directed at personality and stress-prone behavioral patterns.

There have been two principal directions of research into personality and stress: one has concentrated on examining the relationship between various psychological measures (primarily using the Minnesota Multiphasic Personality Inventory [MMPI] and 16 Personality Factory Inventory) and stress-related disease (primarily coronary heart disease); and the other on stress- or coronary-prone behavioral patterns and the incidence of disease (Jenkins, 1971a; 1971b).

Personality Measures

In the first category, there were a number of studies (e.g., Lebovits, Shekelle, and Ostfeld, 1967) which utilized the MMPI. The result of these studies seems to be that before their illness patients with stress-related coronary disease differ from persons who remain healthy on several MMPI scales, particularly those in the "neurotic" triad of hypochondriasis, depression, and hysteria. The occurrence of manifest coronary heart disease (CHD) increases the deviation of patients' MMPI scores further and, in addition, there is ego defense breakdown. As Jenkins (1971a) summarizes: "Patients with fatal disease tend to show greater neuroticism (particularly depression) in prospective MMPI's than those who incur and survive coronary disease." There are three major studies utilizing the 16PF (Bakker, 1967; Finn, Hickey, and O'Doherty, 1969; Lebovits, Shekelle, and Ostfeld, 1967). All three of these report *emotional instability,* particularly for patients with angina pectoris (heart pain that comes on when the oxygen demands on the heart are increased through exercise, emotion, stress, etc.). Two studies report *high conformity and submissiveness* and *low energy/seriousness,* and two report *high self-sufficiency.* Bakker's angina patients are similar to Finn's sample with CHD in manifesting *shyness* and *apprehensiveness.* The results from all three studies portray the patients with CHD or related illness as emotionally unstable and introverted, which is consistent with the MMPI studies. The limitation of these studies is that they are, on balance, retrospective, that is, that anxiety and neuroticism may well be reactions to CHD and other stress-related illnesses rather than precursors of it. Paffenbarger, Wolf, and Notkin (1966) did an interesting prospective study in which they linked university personality information on students with death certificates filed years later. They found a number of significant precursors to fatal CHD, one of which was a high anxiety/neuroticism score for the fatal cases.

Stress Behavioral Patterns

The other research approach to individual stress differences, and the most important from the point of view of prevention, began with the work of Friedman and Rosenman (Friedman, 1969; Rosenman, Friedman, and Strauss, 1964; 1966) in the early sixties and developed later showing a relationship between everyday behavioral patterns of people and their susceptibility to CHD. They found that individuals manifesting certain behavioral traits were significantly more at risk to CHD. These individuals were later referred to as the coronary-prone behavior pattern *Type A* as distinct from *Type B* (low risk of CHD). Type A was found to be the overt behavioral syndrome or style of living characterized by *extremes of competitiveness, striving for achievement, aggressiveness, haste, impatience, restlessness, hyperalertness, explosiveness of speech, tenseness of facial musculature, and feelings of being under pressure of time and under the challenge of responsibility.*

It was suggested that "people having this particular behavioral pattern were often so deeply involved and committed to their work that other aspects of their lives were relatively neglected" (Jenkins, 1971b). In the early studies, persons were designated as Type A or Type B on the basis of clinical judgments of doctors and psychologists or peer ratings. These studies found higher incidence of CHD among Type A than Type B. Many of the inherent methodological weaknesses of this approach were overcome by the classic Western Collaborative Group Study (Rosenman, Friedman, and Strauss, 1964; 1966). It was a prospective national U.S. sample of over 3,400 men free of CHD. All these men were rated Type A or Type B by psychiatrists after intensive interviews, without knowledge of any biological data about them and without the individuals being seen by a cardiologist. Diagnosis was made by an electrocardiographer and an independent medical internist, who were not informed about the subjects' behavioral patterns. They found the following results: after 2½ years of the start of the study, Type-A men between the ages of 39 to 49 and 50 to 59, had 6.5 and 1.9 times respectively the incidence of CHD than Type-B men. They also had a number of symptoms or risk factors of CHD (e.g., raised blood pressure, high cholesterol levels). After 4½ years of the follow-up observation in the study, the *same* relationship of behavioral pattern and incidence of CHD was found. In terms of the clinical manifestations of CHD, individuals exhibiting Type-A behavioral patterns had significantly more incidence of different forms of heart disease. Rosenman, Friedman, and Jenkins (1967) also found that the risk of recurrent CHD was significantly related to Type A characteristics. Quinlan and his colleagues (Quinlan, Burrow, and Hayes, 1969) found the same results among Trappist and Benedictine monks. Monks judged to be Type-A coronary-prone cases (by a double-blind procedure) had 2.3 times the prevalence of angina and 4.3 times the prevalence of heart attacks as compared to monks judged Type B.

Researchers at the Institute of Social Research, University

of Michigan, have focused on A-type characteristics as the sole personality measure in many of their studies. Sales (1969) developed a 49-item questionnaire test of Type A. (A short adaptation of this is available in this book and will be discussed in a later chapter on modifying Type-A behavior.) Using the Sales version, Caplan et al. (1975) found no significant correlations directly between Type-A behavior and various stress measures (e.g., job dissatisfaction, somatic complaints, anxiety, depression, irritation, physical and behavioral "stress" correlates). They found, instead, that Type-A behavior acted as an intervening variable, that is, that in conjunction with work and family stressors it predicted stress-related illness. Caplan and Jones (1975), for example, also reported on the mediating role of personality. In their study of 73 male users of a university computer system in the "stressful" time before a 23-day shutdown, they found confirmation of previous findings that unclear job roles were positively associated with anxiety, depression, and resentment, and that excessive workload was associated with anxiety; however, they reported that these relationships were greatest for Type-A personalities.

In a further study (Caplan, Cobb, and French, 1975), the team investigated the relationship between smoking and A-type personality and shed light on the "A's" ability to modify his coronary-prone behavior. Caplan et al. report that only one-fifth of those who try to give up smoking are successful. Following a questionnaire survey of 200 administrators, engineers, and scientists at NASA, they tried to relate "quitting" (smoking) to job stress, personality, and social support. They found that "quitters" had the lowest levels on quantitative work load, responsibility, and social support and that they scored low on Type-A characteristics. Care must be taken in interpreting these correlational results (it may well be that Type As seek out high workloads, etc.). One conclusion can, however, be drawn unequivocally: A-type personalities are less likely to give up smoking than are B-types (as the authors point out, over time this will lead to an increase in the association between smoking and risk of CHD); thus it would appear that the former's characteristics are so fundamental that they are unable to help themselves—if helped they must be! Payne (1975) has this in mind when he expresses the need (in somewhat rarefied tones) for social systems of trust and support which would "manipulate the degree of environmental pressures so as to give a pin-prick to the comfortable B-types and respite to the harassed As."

Since the early 1970s extensive work has been done on Type-A behavior and job/life stress. Chesney and Rosenman (1980) review a large number of these studies. For example, they found that occupational status and Type-A behavior were related. In a study by Mettlin (1976), for example, 943 white-collar, middle-class males from five different work organizations in Buffalo, New York were investigated. This study population included the administrative and professional staff of a state health agency, an urban utility company's supervisory personnel, officers from industrial and trade unions, a major private university's faculty, and the administrative officers of a large banking corporation. "Not only was the Type-A behavior pattern significantly related to occupational status as measured by rank, level of occupational prestige (as measured by the NORC index), and income, it was also found to be significantly related to *rapid* career achievement as indicated by rank and income relative to age."

In addition, although an indiscriminate comparison of men and women shows that men are significantly more Type A than women, the prevalence of CHD in women was significantly higher for Type As who were employed than for Type-A housewives (Waldron et al., 1978).

To summarize Chesney and Rosenman's conclusion about Type-A behavior: "The Type-A behavior pattern is related to socioeconomic status as defined by occupational prestige, education, and income for both sexes. Further, Type As tend to describe their jobs as having more responsibility, longer hours, and heavier workloads than do Type Bs. Despite these job pressures, Type As in general do not report more job dissatisfaction, anxiety, or depression than do Type Bs. Although the Type-A behavior pattern is correlated with some of the traditional CHD risk factors, it also carries independent risk."

PRESSURE AT WORK

In any job, there are a large number of environmental sources of work stress; the characteristics of the job itself, the role of the person and/or job in the organization, career development pressures, the climate and structure of the organization, the nature of relationships at work, and the problems associated with the interface between the organization and the outside world (e.g., work versus family).

The Job

Stress can be caused by too much or too little work, time pressures and deadlines, having to make too many decisions (see Sofer, 1970), fatigue from the physical strains of the work environment (such as the assembly line), excessive travel, long hours, having to cope with changes at work, and the expenses (monetary and career) of making mistakes (Kearns, 1973). Two factors have received the major part of research effort in this area—working conditions and work overload.

Working Conditions. A great deal of research has been undertaken linking the working conditions of a particular job to physical and mental health. Kornhauser (1965) found, for example, that poor mental health was directly related to unpleasant working conditions, the necessity to work fast and to expend a lot of physical effort, and to excessive and inconvenient hours. There is increasing evidence (Marcson, 1970;

Shepard, 1971) that physical health, as well, is adversely affected by repetitive and dehumanizing environments (e.g., paced-assembly lines). Kritsikis, Heinemann, and Eitner (1968), for example, in a study of 150 men with angina pectoris in a population of over 4,000 industrial workers in Berlin, reported that a larger number of these workers came from work environments employing conveyor-line systems than any other work technology.

Work Overload. French and Caplan (1973) have differentiated overload in terms of *quantitative* and *qualitative* overload. Quantitative refers to having "too much to do," while qualitative means work that is "too difficult." In an early study, French and Caplan (1970) found that objective quantitative overload was strongly linked to cigarette smoking—an important risk factor in coronary heart disease (CHD). Persons with more phone calls, office visits, and meetings per given unit of work time were found to smoke significantly more cigarettes than persons with fewer such engagements. In a study of 100 young coronary patients, Russek and Zohman (1958) found that 25 percent had been working at two jobs, and an additional 45 percent had worked at jobs which required (due to work overload) 60 or more hours per week. They add that although prolonged emotional strain preceded the attack in 91 percent of the cases, similar stress was only observed in 20 percent of the controls. Breslow and Buell (1960) have also reported findings which support a relationship between hours of work and death from coronary disease. In an investigation of mortality rates of men in California, they observed that workers in light industry under the age of 45, who are on the job more than 48 hours a week, have twice the risk of death from CHD compared with similar workers working 40 or less hours a week. Another substantial investigation on quantitative workload was carried out by Margolis, Kroes, and Quinn (1974) on a representative national sample of 1,496 employed persons, 16 years of age or older. They found that overload was significantly related to a number of symptoms or indicators of stress: escapist drinking, absenteeism from work, low motivation to work, lowered self-esteem, and an absence of suggestions to employers.

There is also some evidence that (for some occupations) "qualitative" overload is a source of stress. French, Tupper, and Mueller (1965) looked at qualitative and quantitative work overload in a large university. They used questionnaires, interviews, and medical examinations to obtain data on risk factors associated with CHD for 122 university administrators and professors. They found that one symptom of stress, low self-esteem, was related to overload, but that the pattern was different for the two occupational groupings. Qualitative overload was not significantly linked to low self-esteem among the administrators but was significantly correlated for the professors. The greater the "quality" of work expected of the professor, the lower the self-esteem. Underload can even be a problem, as Heller indicates in his recent novel, *Something Happened:* "I am bored with my work very often now. Everything routine that comes in I pass along to somebody else. This makes my boredom worse. It is a real problem to decide whether it's more boring to do something boring than to pass along everything boring that comes in to somebody else and then have nothing to do at all."

French and Caplan (1973) summarize this research by suggesting that both qualitative and quantitative overload produce at least nine different symptoms of psychological and physical strain: job dissatisfaction, job tension, lower self-esteem, threat, embarrassment, high cholesterol levels, increased heart rate, skin resistance, and more smoking.

Role in the Organization

Another major source of work stress is associated with a person's role at work. A great deal of research in this area has concentrated on role ambiguity and role conflict, since the seminal investigations of the Survey Research Center of the University of Michigan (Kahn, Wolfe, Quinn, Snoek, and Rosenthal, 1964).

Role Ambiguity. Role ambiguity exists when an individual has inadequate information about his work role, that is, where there is *lack of clarity* about the work objectives associated with the role, about colleagues' work expectation of the work role, and about the scope and responsibilities of the job. Kahn et al. (1964) found in their study that men who suffered from role ambiguity experienced lower job satisfaction, high job-related tension, greater futility, and lower self-confidence. French and Caplan (1970) found, at one of NASA's bases, in a sample of 205 volunteer engineers, scientists, and administrators, that role ambiguity was significantly related to low job satisfaction and to feelings of job-related threat to one's mental and physical well-being. This also related to indicators of physiological strain, such as increased blood pressure and pulse rate. Margolis and Kroes (1974) also found a number of significant relationships between symptoms or indicators of physical and mental ill health with role ambiguity in their representative national U.S. sample. The stress indicators related to role ambiguity were depressed mood, lowered self-esteem, life dissatisfaction, job dissatisfaction, low motivation to work, and intention to leave job.

Role Conflict. Role conflict exists when an individual in a particular work role is torn by conflicting job demands or by doing things he/she really does not want to do, or does not think are part of the job specification. The most frequent manifestation of this is when a person is caught between two groups of people who demand different kinds of behavior, or who expect that the job should entail different functions. Kahn et al. (1964) found that men who suffered more role conflict had lower job satisfaction and higher job-related tension. It is interesting to note that they also found that the greater the power or authority of the people "sending" the conflicting role messages, the more role conflict produced job dissatisfaction. This was related to physiological strain as well, as the NASA study illustrates. They telemetered and recorded the heart rate of 22 men for a two-hour period while they were at work in their offices. They found that the mean heart rate for an individual was strongly related to his report of role conflict. A larger and medically more sophisticated study by Shirom, Eden, Silberwasser, and Kellerman (1973) found similar results. Their research is of particular interest because it tries to look simultaneously at a wide variety of potential stressors. They collected data on 762 male kibbutz members aged 30 and above, drawn from 13 kibbutzim throughout Israel. They examined the relationships between coronary heart disease (CHD), abnormal electrocardiographic readings, CHD risk factors (systolic blood pressure, pulse rate, serum cholesterol levels, etc.), and potential sources of work stress (work overload, role ambiguity, role conflict, and lack of physical activity). Their data were broken down by occupational groups—agricultural workers, factory groups, craftsmen, and white-collar workers. It was found that there was a significant relationship between role conflict and abnormal electrocardiographic readings, but for the white-collar workers only. In fact, as we move down the ladder from occupations requiring great physical exertions (e.g., agriculture) to least (e.g., white collar), the greater is the relationship between role ambiguity/conflict and abnormal cardiographic findings. It was also found that as we go from occupations involving excessive physical activities to those with less such activity, CHD increased significantly. Drawing together this material they conclude that clerical, managerial, and professional occupations are more likely to suffer occupational stress from identity and other interpersonal problems, and less from the physical conditions of work.

A more quantified measure of role conflict itself is found

in research reported by Mettlin and Woelfel (1974). They measured three aspects of interpersonal influence—discrepancy between influences, level of influencer, and number of influences—in a study of the educational and occupational aspirations of high-school students. They found that the more extensive and diverse an individual's interpersonal communications network, the more stress symptoms he showed.

The organizational role which is at a boundary—that is, between departments or between the company and the outside world—is, by definition, one of high role conflict. Kahn et al. (1964) have found that such positions are usually highly stressful. Margolis and Kroes (1974), for example, report that foremen are seven times more likely to develop ulcers than shop floor workers.

Responsibility. Another important potential stressor associated with organizational role is "responsibility." One can differentiate here between "responsibility for people" and "responsibility for things" (equipment, budgets, etc.). Wardwell, Hyman, and Bahnson (1964) found that responsibility for people was significantly more likely to lead to CHD than responsibility for things. Increased responsibility for people frequently means that one has to spend more time interacting with others, attending meetings, and, in consequence, as in the NASA study, more time in trying to meet deadline pressures and schedules. Pincherle (1972) also found this in his United Kingdom study of 2,000 executives attending a medical center for a medical check-up. Of the 1,200 managers sent by their companies for their annual examination, there was evidence of physical stress being linked to age and level of responsibility; the older and more responsible the executive, the greater the probability of the presence of CHD risk factors or symptoms. In addition, French and Caplan (1973) found that responsibility for people was significantly related to heavy smoking, diastolic blood pressure, and serum cholesterol levels—the more the individual had "responsibility for things" as opposed to "people" the lower were each of these CHD risk factors.

Relationships at Work

A third major source of stress at work has to do with the nature of relationships with one's boss, subordinates, and colleagues. A number of behavioral scientists (Cooper and Marshall, 1977) have suggested that good relationships between members of a work group are a central factor in individual and organizational health. Nevertheless, very little research work has been done in this area to either support or disprove this hypothesis. French and Caplan (1973) define poor relations as "those which include low trust, low supportiveness, and low interest in listening and trying to deal with problems that confront the organizational member." Both the Kahn et al. and French and Caplan studies came to roughly the same conclusion that mistrust of persons one worked with was positively related to high role ambiguity, inadequate communications between people, and to "psychological strain in the form of low job satisfaction and to feelings of job-related threat to one's well being." As Heller once again illustrates: "In my department, there are six people who are afraid of me, and one small secretary who is afraid of all of us. I have one other person working for me who is not afraid of anyone, not even me, and I would fire him quickly, but I'm afraid of him."

Relationship with Superior. Buck (1972) focused on the attitude and relationship of workers and managers to their immediate boss. When the boss was perceived as "considerate" there was "friendship, mutual trust, respect and a certain warmth between boss and subordinate." He found that those workers who felt that their boss was low on "consideration" reported feeling more job pressure. Workers who were under pressure reported that their boss did not give them criticism in a helpful way, played favorites with subordinates, and "'pulled rank' and took advantage of them whenever they got a chance." Buck concludes that the "lack of considerate behavior of supervisors appears to have contributed significantly to feelings of job pressure."

Relationships with Subordinates. Officially, one of the most critical functions of a manager is his supervision of other people's work. It has long been accepted that an "inability to delegate" might be a problem, but now a new strain is being put on the manager's interpersonal skills—he must learn to govern by participation. Gowler and Legge (1975) point to the factors which may make today's zealous emphasis on participation a cause of resentment, anxiety, and stress for the manager concerned:

1. Mismatch of formal and actual powers.
2. The manager may well resent the erosion of his formal role and powers (and the loss of status rewards).
3. He may be subject to irreconcilable pressures—e.g., to be both participative and to achieve high production.
4. His subordinates may refuse to participate.

Particularly for those with technical and scientific backgrounds (a "things-orientation") personal relationships can be a low priority (seen as "trivial," "petty," "time-consuming," and an impediment to doing the job well), and one would expect their interactions to be more a source of stress than those of people-oriented managers.

Relationships with Colleagues. Besides the obvious factors of office politics and colleague rivalry, we find another element here: stress can be caused not only by the stress of relationships, but also by its opposite—a lack of adequate social support in difficult situations (Lazarus, 1966). At highly competitive managerial levels, for example, it is likely that problem-sharing will be inhibited for fear of appearing weak and much of the American literature (particularly) mentions the "isolated life" of the top executive as an added source of strain. Bob Slocum, the main character in Heller's novel, *Something Happened,* reflected: "I always feel very secure and very superior when I'm sitting inside someone's office with the door closed and other people, perhaps Kagel, or Green, or Brown, are doing all the worrying on the outside about what's going on, on the inside."

Career Development

Two major clusters of potential stressors can be identified in this area: (1) lack of job security—fear of redundancy, obsolescence, or early retirement; and (2) status incongruity (under- or over-promotion), frustration at having reached one's career ceiling.

For many workers their career progression is of overriding importance—by promotion they earn not only money, but also enhanced status and the new job challenges for which they strive. Typically, in the early years at work, this striving and the aptitude to come to terms quickly with a rapidly changing environment is fostered and suitably rewarded by the company. Sofer (1970) found that many of his sample believed that "luck" and "being in the right place at the right time" play a major role. At middle age, and usually middle management levels, career becomes more problematic and most executives find their progress slowed, if not actually stopped. Job opportunities become fewer, those jobs that are available take longer to master, past (mistaken?) decisions cannot be revoked, old knowledge and methods become obsolete, energies may be flagging or demanded for family activities, and there is the press of fresh young recruits to face in competition. Both Levinson (1973) and Constandse (1972)—the latter refers to this phase as *the male menopause*—depict the individual as suffering these fears and disappointments in silent isolation from his family and work colleagues.

The fear of demotion or obsolescence can be strong for those who know they have reached their career ceiling—and most will inevitably suffer some erosion of status before they finally retire. Goffman (1952), extrapolating from a technique employed in the con game ("cooling the mark out"), suggests that the company should bear some of the responsibility for taking the sting out of this (felt) failure experience. As Heller's character Bob Slocum illustrates:

> People in the company are almost never fired; if they grow inadequate or obsolete ahead of schedule, they are encouraged to retire early or are eased aside into hollow, insignificant, newly created positions with fake functions and no authority, where they are sheepish and unhappy for as long as they remain; nearly always, they must occupy a small and less convenient office, sometimes one with another person already in it; or, if they are still young, they are simply encouraged directly (although with courtesy) to find better jobs with other companies and then resign.

From the company perspective, on the other hand, McMurray (1973) puts the case for "not promoting to a higher position" if there is doubt that the employee can fill it. In a syndrome he labels "the executive neurosis," he describes the overpromoted individual as grossly overworking to keep down a top job and at the same time to hide his insecurity—he points to the consequences of this for his work performance and the company. Age is no longer revered as it was—it is becoming a "young man's world." The rapidity with which society is developing (technologically, economically, and socially) is likely to mean that individuals will now need to change careers during their working life (as companies and products are having to do). Such trends breed uncertainty, and research suggests that older workers look for stability (Sleeper, 1975). Unless individuals adapt their expectations to suit new circumstances, career development stress, especially in later life, is likely to become an increasingly common experience.

Organizational Structure and Climate

A fifth potential source of work stress is simply "being in the organization," and the threat to an individual's freedom, autonomy, and identity this poses. Criticisms such as little or no participation in the decision-making process, no sense of belonging, lack of effective consultation and communication, restrictions on behavior (e.g., budgets), and office politics are appropriate here. An increasing number of research investigations are being conducted in this area, particularly into the effect of employee participation in the work place. This research development is contemporaneous to a growing movement in North America and in the EEC countries of worker participation programs, which involve autonomous work groups, worker-directors, and a greater sharing of the decision-making process throughout the organization.

The research more relevant to our interests here, however, is the recent work on lack of participation and stress-related disease. In the NASA study (French and Caplan, 1970), for example, it was found that people who reported greater opportunities for participation in decision making reported significantly greater job satisfaction, low job-related feelings of threat, and higher feelings of self-esteem. Buck (1972) found that both managers and workers who felt "under pressure" most reported that their supervisors "always ruled with an iron hand and rarely tried out new ideas or allowed participation in decision making." Managers who were under stress also reported that their supervisors never let the persons under them do their work in the way they thought best. Margolis, Kroes, and Quinn (1974) found that nonparticipation at work was the most consistent and significant predictor or indicator of strain and job-related stress. They found that nonparticipation was significantly related to the following health risk factors: overall poor physical health, escapist drinking, depressed mood, low self-esteem, low life satisfaction, low job satisfaction, low motivation to work, intention to leave job, and absenteeism from work. Kasl (1973) also found that low job satisfaction was related to nonparticipation in decision making, inability to provide feedback to supervisors, and lack of recognition for good performance; and that poor mental health was linked to close supervision and no autonomy at work (Quinn, Seashore, and Mangione, 1971).

Extra-Organizational Sources of Stress

The sixth and final "source" of external job stress is more a "catch-all" for all those exchanges between his life outside and his life inside the organization that might put pressure on an individual—family problems (Pahl and Pahl, 1971), life crises (Cooper and Marshall, 1977), financial difficulties, conflict of personal beliefs with those of the company, and the conflict of company with family demands. Despite repeated calls for researchers to acknowledge that the individual "functions as a totality" (Wright, 1975), the practical problems of encompassing the whole person in one research plan usually leave those who try with either incomprehensibly complex results or platitudinous generalizations. Most studies, then, have only one life area as the focus of study.

The individual worker has two main problems vis-à-vis his family. The first is that of time- and commitment-management. Not only does his busy life leave him few resources to cope with other people's needs, but in order to do his job well, the individual usually also needs support from others to cope with the "background" details of house management, etc., to relieve stress when possible, and to maintain contact with the outside world. The second, often a result of the first, is the spillover of crises or stresses in one system to affect the other.

THE DEVELOPMENT OF THE DUAL-CAREER FAMILY: ITS IMPACT ON THE FAMILY AND ORGANIZATIONAL LIFE

One of the most significant developments on family life in the last two decades has been the emancipation of women, equal opportunities and affirmative action legislation, and its accompanying movement toward "dual-career families." It is this phenomenon that we must begin to understand if we are to minimize the pressures we are currently seeing on the family unit and in organizational life. Today, family stress is to a large extent a product of the lack of planning and foresight in the wake of social change. Individuals, families, and work organizations have not adequately planned for the increasing desire of women to both work and have a family; it is this social myopia which has led to increasing evidence of families under pressure, e.g., divorce, separation, delinquency, etc.

Consequences of Dual-Career Marriages

Since the dual-career marriage is slowly but surely becoming a part of Western life, it is worth noting the consequences it is likely to have on the marital relationship, the children, society, and business. The viewpoints regarding this are mixed.

Gloomy Predictions. Back in 1954, Parsons (1954) prophesized the self-destructive nature of dual-career marriages and stated that marriage between professionals was "not a workable way of emancipating most American married women from domesticity." He based this on the sociocultural reason that this type of marriage could throw the wife into destructive role competition with her husband. Indeed, high stress levels are experienced by many dual-career families. Pahl (1971) suggested that there is an "infection exhaustion" caused by the strain and bustle dual-career couples are subject to. The stress that is internal to the partnership derives primarily from role conflict, since the dual-career couples must function satisfactorily in three roles simultaneously. "Identity" crises are caused because of the difficulties of overcoming the societal norms of "housework and family rearing" being *feminine,* and "work" being *masculine.* Role cycling dilemmas arise from organizational problems at crucial stages. Role cycling stress, which comes about at job transition points, results in dual-career couples trying to avoid having to deal with more than one of the three areas of engagement being in transition at the same time. Many of them become well established in their careers before having children. Stress also results when one partner's career progresses in such a way as to conflict with the others, such as promotions for one spouse which involves a job relocation which could result in a break in the other spouse's career (Rapoport and Rapoport, 1971).

The dual-career couple's social life tends to be restricted, since they have to cope jointly with both the responsibilities of work and home. This results in their rationing out their social life and modifying their choice of friends. In the case of relatives, however, the choice cannot be made that easily and this causes many dilemmas socially, particularly to the wife, since the dual-career husband tends to be close to his mother and is unable to ration his visits to her (Bebbington, 1973).

A questionnaire given to 137 girls and 92 boys from intact families suggests that parents and children disagree over a wide range of issues more often when the mother works (Tropman, 1968). Brofenbrenner's (1977) misgivings about the family in which both parents work revolve around his concern for the effect it could have on children who return home from school in the evening to empty houses. These children, he feels, "search out other children in similar situations and create a peer group culture which will probably be an ugly one"—of destruction, breaking, and acting out. All over America—where dual-career families are becoming the norm—schools can be seen dealing with problems of vandalism and violence. The frightening thing is its implication, namely, that a major institution responsible for preparing the next generation for adulthood is a focus of pointless destruction (Byre, 1977).

There is a mass of research which points to the variety of stresses and strains of the changing family structure. For example, Staines et al. (1979) found in a large scale study of dual-career families that husbands of working wives reported they wished they had married somebody else and thought of divorce more frequently than husbands of housewives. Instead of detailing the voluminous research evidence on the negative impact of the changing nature of marriage, it might be useful to assess the problems currently being faced by different marriages at different stages in their life cycle.

Profile of Wives

In Figure 2.1 we present a schematic representation of the variety of current roles played by wives in Western society at different stages of the life cycle, together with a discussion of how these roles not only affect the wives but also their husbands and the organizations they work for. (This was developed by myself and Dr. Judi Marshall of Bath University, UK.) We are talking here primarily of white-collar employees because they seem to be the ones experiencing the greatest stress—because of the increased mobility of their well-educated and increasingly professionally trained wives. This is not to indicate that problems don't exist for blue-collar families, but for historical reasons (they have been working longer in female-type jobs) are less dramatic and destructive (Cooper and Marshall, 1977). Our typology of wives' roles is organized along two axes; one represents a time dimension from the past to the future, while the other represents the family life cycle from "early marriage" through "childbearing and rearing" to the "empty

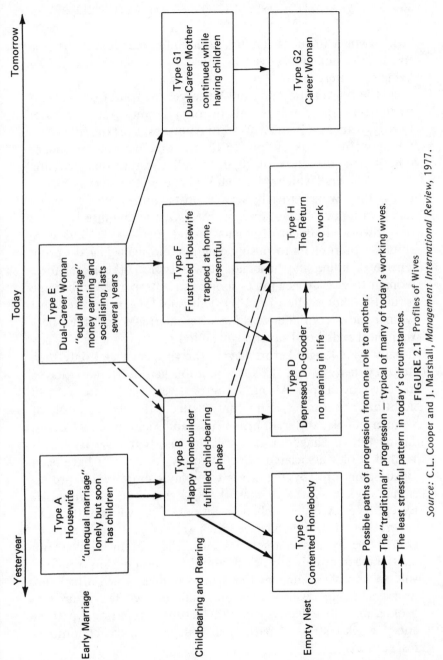

FIGURE 2.1 Profiles of Wives

Source: C.L. Cooper and J. Marshall, *Management International Review*, 1977.

35

nest" (which includes families with children at home but relatively independent, as well as those with children married or living separately).

The time continuum from Yesteryear to Tomorrow is meant to illustrate the developments in role relations over time. Over twenty years ago, in most Western countries, most (middle-class) young women took on jobs to fill the time between secondary school and the start of their "true" vocation—married life. Those "careers" which were followed had no long-term expectations; they were basically service posts (nurse, teacher, secretary), with poor promotional prospects, did not require excessive out-of-work hours involvement as did men's jobs, and were suitable forerunners to raising children and managing the problems of a home and husband. It was typical, therefore, for a woman to give up her job as soon as she got married to become a full-time housewife (Type A). This is no longer the case. Most women now continue working after marriage and thus help their husbands build up enough capital to "start a home." They usually wait longer before having the first child and only then do they leave work. This "generation gap" differentiation is depicted by Types A and E, respectively, in Figure 2.1. In addition, this time axis not only reflects the changing role of women but also different generations and socioeconomic status. In the United Kingdom, it is still the case that seniority is age-related. Roles associated with Types A to D are or have been filled, therefore, by the wives of today's more senior professional workers—those in the 50 to 65 year old age group; all except Type A are possible descriptions of the wives of the next generation of white-collar workers (although a small number still fit the Type A characterization). The thin lines and arrows on the diagram indicate possible paths of progression from one role to another. Some of the many variables which affect this progression are dealt with more fully below. The heavy unbroken and dotted lines show the accepted traditional pattern and the least stressful pattern in today's changed conditions, respectively.

So far, we have concentrated on the role alternatives open to women in a family. We should now like to put these in a wider context of the mapping of role relationships in a marriage, and the effects that this is likely to have on the husband at work and, through him, the organization which employs him. Viewed against the background of Figure 2.1, what most organizations demand and expect of their white-collar employees in return for success and promotion has not changed dramatically over the last thirty years. (It must be noted that here we assume that most professionals view their jobs as major sources of life satisfaction and are sufficiently ambitious to follow a developing, expanding, and fulfilling career throughout their working lives—we are, therefore, concentrating on the man who wants to "get on".) Organizations expect their white-collar employees to become highly involved in the success of the company and of their job in particular. They are expected to display their involvement and dedication by heavy investments of emotional energy and time, working in the evenings and on weekends when necessary, traveling on company business, spending "appropriate" time on work-related (usually "stag") social activities and responding enthusiastically to company offers of promotion or geographic mobility. Any free time they do have should be spent in rest and recuperation to enable them to come back refreshed and ready for further company service.

We should now like to discuss some of the possible ways in which these demands and the potential wife's roles might interact.

Type A: The Housewife. While we feel this is a dying breed of woman, it is necessary to elaborate some of its aspects as background to C, D, and H below. The main problems of *The Housewife* are loneliness and boredom. Typically, she has not received as much higher education as her husband and is likely to accept the role of wife and mother as "what she was born for." Marriage was usually not as exciting and fulfilling as she had expected and sooner or later a job move for her husband took her away from supportive family and friends, and she was left friendless in a foreign and often slightly hostile society. While she might complain of neglect, particularly at the time her husband devoted to building up his career, and be jealous of the exciting, challenging job for which he left her every morning (especially any traveling), the housewife's attitude to her husband was basically very supportive and her husband usually found her cooperative and able to give him individual attention when he wanted it. This is not to say that she was not unhappy at times but fundamentally she accepted her role, subscribed to the Protestant work ethic, considered herself lucky when she looked back at the hard days of the Depression, and looked forward to starting a family.

Type B: Happy Homebuilder. The phase of *Happy Homebuilder* is an extremely important one for a woman, especially for those who have no other career ambitions. It is a time for exploring and establishing an extremely fulfilling but demanding and time-consuming role. The young wife's preoccupation now parallels her husband's involvement in his job. This phase is one of relatively few problems. The couple's relationship is, however, likely to be somewhat distanced and their roles highly differentiated, and for many this will mean that psychologically they don't meet very often. As with the other facets of their lives, the couple are likely to keep many of their problems separate. Because he wants to preserve a "safe haven" in which to shut out work matters, and because much of his job will be too confidential and technical for "her to understand," the manager tends not to bring his work stresses home to his wife. She, in turn, will keep many of her own problems to herself in order to protect him from extra strain, to avoid negative feedback, to preserve his image of her as a loving and supportive wife, and in addition, because their time together is too precious to waste. She may also buffer him from the demands of the children ("Daddy's tired, leave him alone, now") and the organizational aspects of running a home (e.g., house moving, arranging holidays, organizing house repairs, etc.). By protecting each other in this way, the working husband and his wife are also shielding themselves from having to share and handle the stresses of the other. Thus, each is deeply involved in deriving satisfaction from his/her *own* separate world, and their shared pleasures are mainly when they "meet" through their children. The husband is free to devote himself to work, and his wife's activities and behavior directly support him in this by providing a stable, comfortable home, a ready-made and undemanding low-stress identity system (*husband* and *father*) and, in addition, local social contacts (often, again, via the children). This is a life of "complementary" rather than "shared" relationships.

Type C and D: Contented Homebody and Depressed Do-Gooder. If the wife is willing to continue to maintain a supportive role vis-à-vis her husband, as the children become more independent and move away from home, we would describe her as a *Contented Homebody.* As her family duties decrease she may well take on outside activities—voluntary social work, tennis, painting, and the like—as keeping house (particularly compared to her previous levels of activity) is by no means a full-time job. Particularly if her husband has done well in his career (e.g., Chief Executive, Senior Partner, etc.), she may well take on a social role in relation to his job—entertaining visitors, acting as a resource for his subordinates' wives, providing a social focus for his department, etc. If she adopts the latter type of role she is likely to derive much of her social identity from her husband's status. In this type of marriage the couple continue in their complementary roles, he is often extremely successful at work, and many would say that the organization has benefited by getting one and a half employees for the price of one.

Behaviorally it is not easy to distinguish the *Contented Homebody* from the potential role we have labeled *Depressed Do-Gooder.* Basically, they fill their days in the same ways but the latter does not find the things she does fulfilling. Often she will pick up and drop a series of hobbies and local community activities looking for one to give her life "meaning"—but without success. Usually, too, she is prevented from getting a "proper" job as a possible outlet (input?) because she has no marketable job skills or lacks the confidence and training opportunities to resurrect any she did have, and also because both she and her husband have been brought up to believe that "he should support her."

How then do the *Contented Homebodies* and the *Depressed Do-Gooders* come to differ so radically in their outlook on life? Consistently we find that while the former has built up a meaningful identity, the latter has failed to do so. There could be various reasons for this—perhaps raising a family was not a sufficient accomplishment for her, perhaps geographic moves or upward social mobility have disrupted her life and prevented her from becoming integrated into a meaningful social society, or perhaps she has not been able to derive meaning from her husband's work. Whatever the reasons, the wife in these circumstances is likely to be unhappy and frequently depressed. Though she may turn to her husband for support he may well be in no position to help her—if his job is still demanding he will not have the time or energy to spare for his wife's rather vague identity problems, or it may be that his development also shows signs of slackening pace (i.e., he may have reached his "career ceiling") and is facing the problem of lack of meaning in his life too. Such a couple are likely to find these circumstances extremely stressful, particularly if they developed a rather distanced relationship in their earlier married life; they may now be hampered by their lack of experience in dealing with interpersonal problems of this nature.

Types E, F, G, and H: Dual-Career Woman, Frustrated Housewife, Dual-Career Mother, The Return to Work. A common characteristic of the women who fill these roles is their high level of formal further education and their tendency to seek satisfaction in work outside the home. In Type E, for example—today's predominant pattern—we find that the white-collar husband has typically married someone with a university degree whom he met at college rather than the "girl back home" whom we saw taking on the role of *Housewife*. During early marriage the couple both work, but we find variations in the women's attitude to her job. For some their job soon takes second place to their husband and home, they value it more as a way of accumulating capital and for the fact that they will be able to "take it up" again after accomplishing the immediate central aim of raising a family. This reduced involvement is often seen in a decision to change to part-time working or a willingness to take up a lower level, less time-consuming job following a geographic move. This woman has chosen to adopt a supportive role in relation to her husband's work and will make sacrifices in order to help him further his career. In addition, when the couple decide to start a family these wives will probably become *Happy Homebuilders*.

At the other extreme, we have the true dual-career orientation: both partners are heavily involved in their jobs and the wife continues working because it is important to her to do so. If asked, she would undoubtedly say that she was a "teacher" rather than subscribe to a *derived identity* from her role as wife. Their home-building is, rather than "nest preparation," the organization of a base of operations for separate careers and joint social activities. The success of this type of role relationship will depend on two basic issues. First, the relative importance the woman attaches to her job, her husband's job, and home maintenance; second, and interactively, the husband's expectations of a "wife." A consistent complaint of husbands whose wives worked (at other life stages as well as this one) is that their wives became "too involved" in the jobs they did. The working woman is in a position of obvious role conflict, especially if her job makes demands on her after 5:00 P.M. and thus interferes temporarily with her role as housekeeper and companion. The increasing numbers of women attending a university has made this more likely; no longer are they necessarily secretaries and the like, with limited hours and responsibilities. Their career opportunities may now extend to market research, computer analysis, managerial positions, etc., just like their husbands, and the norms and expectations in these occupations are the same as those discussed above for men. "Equal opportunities" are generally only open to women who show themselves willing to subscribe to these norms.

The repercussions in the marriage of these role conflicts will depend largely on the husband's attitudes and behavior. We believe that a relatively *New Man* is necessary to understand and accommodate a *New Woman*'s ambitions. This *New Man* must be willing to sacrifice home comforts (the "home" he has come to expect from his own parental pattern), share the burden of home maintaining activities and, most important, be able to cope with a wife who may well be successful in a world which bears comparison to his. While the roles, for example, of Manager and Wife/Mother are complementary (and enhance each other if they are both performed well), the roles of Manager and (female) Advertising Agency Executive can be competitive (either by salary or status differentials), and it is not easy for one to do well without being a potential threat to the other.

Many men now subscribe to the *New Man* ethic and show pride in their "clever mates'" achievements; the behaviors of most, however, show signs of an underlying ambivalence. Few are truly happy to earn less than their wives, most positively reinforce "good cooking" and "housekeeping" while denying the importance of such things, and most are happy to be "fussed over" (in moderation), but openly affirm the "equalitarian living mate" ideal. Ronald Laing, among other British psychiatrists, has put forward strong evidence that the reception of conflicting messages from highly valued and inescapable sources plays a part in the etiology of schizophrenia. Perhaps this explains the confusion about life goals of many of today's young women.

Whatever his success in coping with these interpersonal issues at home, the working professional husband in this situation is less likely to be able to devote as much of himself to his work as did members of the previous generation. If he is a true *New Man* he will, by definition, value and spend time on "his share" of the household duties; the couple will probably also develop a pattern of sharing each other's work pressures and satisfactions as part of their emphasis on a joint lifestyle. If he is an *Ambivalent New Man* he is likely to find the role negotiations required to maintain his marriage both energy-consuming and distracting. Both alternatives are far from the previous pattern in which the husband was released from duties and buffered from pressure so that he could get on with his career. The egalitarian nature of operations in this type of marriage dictates that decisions should be made jointly and with the aim of maximizing the satisfaction of both partners. This causes particularly acute problems when the couple is faced with demands from his organization (and in the future, hers as well), for example, the offer of a geographic move or a period of foreign travel. No longer can the husband accept and *then* go home and tell his wife. Many organizations have not yet appreciated the ramifications of this development and still negotiate doggedly with only one member of the decision-making unit. This immediately puts the employee in a conflict situation and will add to any strain he already feels at not being his own boss.

Returning now to the wife's conflicts: in the long-term she must decide how important it is for her to pursue her career relative to having children. While many women "solve" their problem by acknowledging a "felt need" to bear and raise children and therefore drop out of their careers to become *Happy Homebuilders* (usually planning to return to work later), some take on the role of mother only to deeply regret their action later. It is such women who are potential *Frustrated Housewives;* they are not happy with the role of mother and housekeeper in which they find themselves. It is not, generally, that these women have been tricked into motherhood by unwanted pregnancy—they have usually decided to have children because they feel that they might find it satisfying or that they might later regret not having done so, or in response to social pressure from parents, friends, or husband. Once there, they are trapped—they are well-educated enough to have known about the effects of parental neglect on younger children and have high standards in their mother roles; few would even consider working before their children are five years old, and many feel that they should wait until their children are of secondary school age (twelve years old). Even if they would like to work, many have careers which cannot be pursued part-time or which necessitate living near a major city. Not only do these women derive little intrinsic enjoyment from the day-to-day activities of running a home and raising a family, but they feel that they are actually suffering from the experience. Without the intellectual and social stimulations of the jobs they know they are capable of and happy doing, they feel that they are in danger of becoming "vegetables." The task of bringing up children, by its very nature, is a constant battle against overwhelming odds and most mothers feel that they perform badly—for the thwarted career woman, particularly, being a mother may *not* be an adequately meaningful identity.

There is little positive action the *Frustrated Housewife* can take and usually she directs her negative feelings at the nearest target—her husband. He has everything she lacks and also reaps the benefits of her grudging labors. She is jealous of his work and *any* time he devotes to it (she may well resent him working late or socializing after work, for example); she will discourage him from bringing work home, either physically or psychologically (as a problem or a triumph), and she will certainly be loath to play the "social dutiful wife" role, which in some organizations is essential to his career progress. The husband facing this type of home situation is justified in feeling that he too is trapped. However sympathetic he may be and as much as he tries to supply continuous support, there are no easy practical solutions to his wife's problems. The strain this imposes on him, at what might well be a crucial career time, is considerable and may seriously affect his work performance. Problems with relationships at home are likely to effect work in the following ways: (a) tensions are dissipated in relationships at work, (b) cramming work into a nine-to-five day to avoid bringing work home, thereby creating work overload, (c) career decision making affected by his wife's hostility toward his work (e.g., refusing to move for promotion or objecting to his taking on greater responsibilities or travel commitments). It would not be surprising in the admittedly extreme situation we have depicted for the husband to partly lose patience with his wife's frustrations and send her "stress messages" in his turn: "Life would be a lot simpler if I didn't have a wife and family."; "You were a much nicer person to know when you were out at work." (a particularly cutting comparison); "It's not surprising that I prefer to spend time at work rather than listening to your moaning."

Sadly, "time" rather than "active coping" seems the easiest solution to the problems of couples in this role tangle. The husband misses career advancement opportunities and compensates by reducing his ambitions and putting his family first in importance; as children grow up the wife becomes freer to look outside the home for meaningful activities. But there are signs that changes in society are helping to alleviate some of the problems: "flexi-time" allows many employees to tailor their work hours to fit home demands; some firms are employing two people to cover one job so that two women can cooperate to share the tasks of working and child-minding. In Britain, for example, local groups belonging to The National Housewives Register organize activities for young mothers who prefer not to talk about the problems of washing diapers; "babysitting circles" free couples from the home more regularly; and local colleges offer interesting and mind-developing courses in everything from pottery to the degree subjects that will help in the resumption of (paid) work in later life.

These measures are all aimed at making the sacrifices a

career woman undertakes in this phase more palatable. An alternative, however, is to obviate the need for sacrifices altogether by following a continuous dual-career progression—with short interruptions for child bearing. In this phase we see many of the problems discussed above for the newly married dual-career state, but with some added complications. First, child-rearing (unlike dish washing) cannot be neglected without risking serious repercussions. To date there have been no large-scale developments of adequate surrogate care facilities in many countries. Second, the woman's decision to continue, rather than break and resume her work, means that she is as able to sucessively develop a career as is her husband, which intensifies the problem of her time/involvement management and his susceptibility to feeling threatened by her competition. Third, compared to the household of the *Frustrated Housewife* in which the norm is that the husband's job should be denied importance and underperformance is therefore encouraged, the husband of a career woman is likely to be expected to place a high emphasis on his work, devote time to it, and succeed. In this situation the husband could well push himself more at work, courting the strain of overpromotion. Unlike the husband of the *Happy Homebuilder,* hers will lack the backup of a supportive wife with plenty of time to help him cope with work stresses (she may well have plenty of her own) and a ready-made social world in which he can unwind. It may also become important not to be "left behind" if his wife is successful. Fourth, sheer limited capacity problems may well mean that the couple adopts a slightly "distanced" relationship similar to that seen in Type B (*Happy Homebuilder*), but without the tacitly agreed priorities of this latter Type; decision making in the dual-career family could, therefore, be a traumatically divisive activity. Personality characteristics will play a large part in the success or otherwise of this type of marriage—the benefits of a family pattern which simultaneously satisfies the needs of all its members are obvious. If, however, the couple are both achievement-oriented and conscientious, they may well take on more than they can jointly manage.

Type H: The Return to Work. During the "empty nest" phase, some women return to work. This could be at any point in time when she feels that her family is sufficiently able to cope with such a development, and may well be part-time at first to fit in with their demands. Trends towards smaller families (to release women earlier) and the fact that many middle-aged women are robbed of most of extended families duties because their offspring, in turn, are highly mobile, have helped to make an early return to work increasingly more likely. Other motivating reasons may be the desire to supplement the family income, a need for achievement and satisfaction, or an attempt to maintain a separate life to compensate for a husband too dedicated to *his* work.

The relational implications of The Return depend largely on which Type the couple have progressed from. The *Happy Homebuilder* may initially have difficulty because she was not sufficiently interested in education, when younger, to acquire marketable skills. If, however, she can overcome such problems both she and her husband are likely to benefit. Typically, she will guard against her job intruding in any way on the supportive pattern she and her husband have built up, and as long as she does this—maintaining his job as their joint prime consideration—he can only gain from her added interest in life. One husband remarked, in a recent study, how pleased he was to see his wife enjoying her job so much: "She re-became the woman I married." This "New Wife" may later play an important part as a "sharer" of activities as her husband nears retirement and his job demands less of his energies.

For the wife who does not limit her work activities to fit in with home demands, the situation is likely to be more difficult, especially if her husband has come to expect a particularly high level of home comfort. Continuous dual-career families will have negotiated these demarcation issues earlier; previous *Happy Homebuilders* are likely to experience some initial friction, but as we said earlier, the husband's needs usually take priority in any conflict situation such as this. It is the *Frustrated Housewife* who is likely to be the most excessive in her demands for work satisfaction. The couple for whom this is true are likely to undergo yet another period of turmoil as they attempt to establish a new balance in their relationship. The husband now has some hope of favorable outcomes and looks forward to the release of previous tensions. His wife, however, is likely to be under considerable strain as she reenters the world of work, of which she has high expectations of satisfactions, which may not be fully met by the local labor market. Provided that these boundary issues can be successfully worked out, the wife's return to work is likely to be beneficial to both partners.

Thusfar, our discussion has described effects *in general.* Figure 2.2 summarizes these generalizations in a "Who Wins" table for the three main actors—the husband, his wife, and the husband's employing organization. "Winning" essentially means the matching of expectations and needs, whatever these may be, with reality.

We see that while the traditional marriage progression (A → B → C) might lack some of the personal contact and growth elements advocated today, overall it was beneficial to both partners and to the company. In it, relationships were fundamentally in balance. The marriage patterns of today's white-collar husbands, however, contain inherent conflicts and ambiguities, which mean that equilibrium must be established and individually, by negotiation, rather than taken for granted. While the bonds arrived at between husband and wife have the potential to be exceedingly rich and rewarding, their establishment and maintenance does require an expenditure of energy on the husband's part not previously demanded. In many cases his organization will find him less able, and probably less willing, to devote himself wholeheartedly to its goals in the short term.

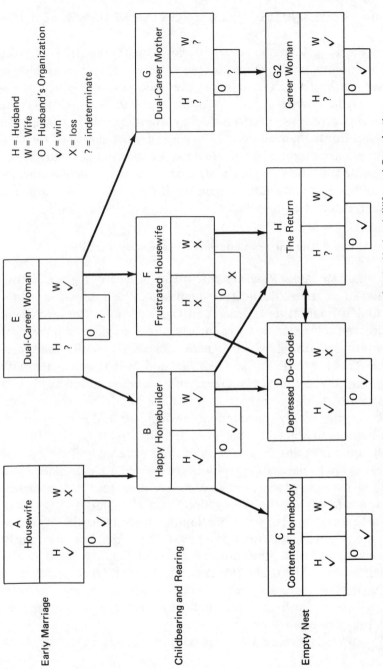

FIGURE 2.2 "Who Wins" Table: Wives' Roles and Win/Loss Consequences for the Husband, Wife, and Organization

Source: C.L. Cooper and J. Marshall, *Management International Review*, 1977.

49

In the long term, however, it may reap the benefits of more harmonious family relationships. As Hannah Gavron suggests in her book, *The Captive Wife,* the social change which is encouraging women to play a more active role in industrial life creates problems, particularly "by advancing more quickly on some fronts than others." She concludes her survey of the conflicts currently being experienced by housebound but work-oriented mothers: "What is needed above all is some deliberate attempt to re-integrate women in all their many roles with the central activities in society."

Favorable Consequences of Dual-Career Families

On the Marital Relationship. Instead of destroying the institution of marriage, dual-career families may well cause a strengthening of marital ties (Orden and Orden, 1969). The increase in the employment of wives brings about a more symmetrical family structure in which a greater degree of equality could prevail between husband and wife (Blood, 1965). When the wife works, the couple's resources tend to be equalized, which in turn affects the power structure of the family. We see a "companionship family" developing in which the husband pays more attention to what his wife says, and she begins to treat him as an equal instead of "putting him on a pedestal." The effect of this is that relatively her power grows, while his declines. This companionship family may well be a new stage in the history of the family in the West (Blood and Hamblin, 1958). These dual-career couples act more jointly in directing their internal responsibilities and tend to choose their friends more jointly as compared with traditionally oriented families. Even in the pessimistic Ohio study (Cohen, 1973), confidence was felt in the ties of mutual trust which developed in the marital relationship as both husband and wife participated increasingly in the decision making.

When the wife starts working, husbands start helping in

the house (Powell, 1963). This change in the household division of labor comes about because it becomes extremely difficult for a woman employed full-time to take care of all the housework. Though the husband should ideally take over an increasingly equal share of the household duties, he rarely does so. Nevertheless, he still does more than he would normally do under the traditional family arrangement (Ostapen, 1971).

Arnott (1972, 1977) studied 235 dual-career couples, from which she too felt that marriage in America is not threatened by the increasing trend towards "independence" and "careers for women." Relationships tended to be more direct, adult, and honest. Progressive involvement in careers was planned by those couples who had children. The shared interests which result should, Arnott feels, help avoid a break in understanding between the couple in the "empty nest" years. In fact, marital and family problems resulting from the pressure of intimate interdependencies of the nuclear family could decrease. Instead of breaking up, Western family life is being reshaped slowly and thoroughly, though not painlessly, of course.

The intensity of a woman's involvement in the labor force and the degree of her success is often influenced by her husband's attitude. In Arnott's study of women and their husbands, it was found that husbands' pride in their wives' achievement and individuality worked in counterpoint with the autonomy of wives and higher tolerance for tension of the couples, to help minimize the strain of transition. In fact, husbands were more keen on getting their wives to become involved in careers than the women themselves. Ginzberg (1966) too found that among educated women who were capable of independence and interested in careers, their husbands' attitude was often decisive in whether and to what degree they pursued careers. In a study of academic women, Bernard (1964) found that careers of married, academic women depend largely on their husbands. Cussler (1958) too reported that several women executives had married men who were proud of their careers. In an attitude study of executives, several women respondents who were in top management positions made references to help given to them by husbands earlier in their careers as the key to success in the new kind of double life. Their husbands' support and understanding provided the necessary factor for a good adjustment (Bowman, Beatrice, and Greyser, 1965).

Martin et al. (1975) tested the Parsonian hypothesis predicting the disruptive consequences of professional marriages, in a five-year longitudinal study, and found that the wife gains professional advantages in occupationally specific dual-career marriages. There was a superior success pattern of sociologist wives studied as compared with other females in the profession. The findings denied Parson's early scepticism and went in favor of the alternative that marrying professional colleagues entails "fertile interaction between the couple" relevant to the profession, thus contributing to the success and development of the wife's career.

On the Children. The employment of the mother has an effect on her children but does not necessarily foster destructive impulses in society as thought by Bronfenbrenner. The same sort of role convergence that takes place between husband and wife can be seen between son and daughter too. Daughters of working mothers are more self-sufficient, independent, and disobedient (Siegel et al., 1963). Seeing their mother work, according to Siegel et al. encourages daughters to take up part-time and summer employment. They do this while at the same time increasing their share of the housework. Seeing the females in their family becoming more equal with them, however, somehow has the effect of demoralizing sons in the short run. In a way, this can be explained by the fact that they are modeling their fathers in no longer feeling responsible for providing monetary support for the family (Blood, 1965). The boys tend to become more meek and obedient, as Hoffman (1963) suggests, reflecting the lower status of their fathers. In other words, the boys become less masculine and the girls become more masculine (Blood, 1965), none of which are undesirable trends, but merely bring about role convergence and increase equality among the sexes.

Advantages have been found to accrue to children when the mother works. Working women are less demanding on their children since they have devoted less time and effort in bringing them up. Moreover, children no longer have to feel guilty about their mother sacrificing everything for them, in terms of a career (Zajur and Ocio, 1972). The attitudes towards female employment are also favorably affected by the incidence of the mother working. A study (Tropman, 1968) of 1,055 ninth-grade children in the United States, revealed that those whose mothers worked looked upon this employment as less of a threat to the marriage relationship than did children of nonworking mothers. This effect was found to be more significant for males than for females. To sum up, we can say that the employment of the mother leads to a convergence of roles of the husband and wife, and of son and daughter, whereby they all participate more in common activities and share in a closer family life.

Effects of Managerial Attitudes Towards Dual Careers

One major barrier to women trying to play an effective, stressless dual role could be the managerial stereotype regarding the appropriate role for women in society. This is probably because managers regard the main female role as that of a helpful supportive wife. This type of managerial attitude could result in subtle discriminatory practices, which could have an influence on a woman's adjustment to a dual role. Discriminatory practices in organizations are geared toward avoiding the disturbance of a working woman's married life. This is achieved by not putting her in jobs with heavy travel commitments or which require transfers to other areas or which need a lot of dedication, assuming that the women were not capable of giving their jobs priority over their family. On top of this, managers expect that women will help further their husbands' careers by accompanying them to business functions, etc., but do not expect this to be reciprocated by their husbands. This situation could cause frustration to a working wife, and when she compares her situation with that of her husband, marital envy and strain could set in.

In fact, an attitude study of 2,000 executives revealed that the home-job syndrome was quoted most often as the major obstacle to women's success in management (Bowman, Beatrice, and Greyser, 1965).

Conclusions

The conclusions we can perhaps infer from this review are as follows. Societal and environmental factors have led to an increase in the number of women in the workforce who are becoming more qualified and striving for higher positions in their jobs. Many of these women are married, as a result of which the dual-career family emerges as a new stage in the pattern of Western family life.

Dual-career spouses tend to have distinct background characteristics. They tend to be "only" or eldest children, to have had working mothers and stressful experiences in their childhood. In fact, stress plays an integral part in the establishment of the dual-career family.

In spite of gloomy predictions regarding the self-destructiveness of dual-career marriages, there is a body of evidence to show this may not be so. Dual-career marriages have been shown to lead to equalization of roles between husband and wife and son and daughter, and bring about a closeness in the family.

The success of a woman's adjustment to her dual role is influenced greatly by both her husband's and her boss's attitude.

Most of the empirical research on the dual-career situation focuses on the reasons why women adopt dual roles and the effect it has on their families. Little attention has been given on how to make a dual-career lifestyle work. In addition, the effect dual-career roles will have on organizational life has not been fully examined. The adjustment organizations will have to make in accommodating needs of dual-career couples in fundamental attitude changes, in providing flexible working hours, in the introduction of day-care centers in the workplace, etc., are areas in dire need of action. These are issues we will be dealing with in Chapter 7.

The Costs of Stress to Society

chapter 3

Stress is a topical subject. There is no escaping its increasing coverage in both popular (e.g., Heller's *Something Happened*) and academic literature. It has been suggested that this "popularity" may be because, as a concept, it integrates several previously distinct fields of social science study (McGrath, 1970), or more cynically, that it is the result of a "bandwagon effect" (Appley, 1964). A simpler and more easily supported possibility is that it is a topic of direct relevance to a large proportion of the inhabitants of today's Western industrial world (as the release of tension which typically accompanies its open discussion convincingly shows). Public and government concern is increasing as the short- and long-term effects of stress for the individual, his family, the company he works for, and even the national economy are being realized. Let us look, briefly, at the "accounting" that can be done at each of these levels.

For the individual, stress means "human suffering"—short-term discomfort and unhappiness, but with the possibility of long-term disease. There is a substantial body of health literature (Cooper and Payne, 1978) which documents those effects of relevance in the home and workplace—anxiety, inability to concentrate, irritability, minor physical ailments, etc. Hinkle (1973) is among the majority who believe that these initial signs and symptoms lead to longer-term, incapacitating diseases:

> Thus the potential magnitude of the effects (of reactions to the environment) appears to be as great as the effects which can be produced by any other influences upon these processes, not even excluding those which destroy or permanently damage the systems that are involved in them.

Stress-related illnesses such as coronary heart disease have been on the steady upward trend over the past couple of decades in the United States and the United Kingdom. In England and Wales, for example, the death rate in men between 35 and 44 nearly doubled between 1950 and 1973 and has increased much more rapidly than that of older age ranges (for example, 45 to 54). By 1973, forty-one percent of all deaths in the age group 35 to 44 were due to cardiovascular disease, with nearly 30 percent due to cardiac heart disease. In fact, in 1976 the American Heart Association estimated the cost of cardiovascular disease in the U.S. at $26.7 billion a year. In addition to the more extreme forms of stress-related illnesses, there has been an increase in other possible stress manifestations such as alcoholism, where admissions to alcoholism units in U.K. hospitals increased from roughly under 6,000 in 1966 to over 8,000 in 1974; and industrial accidents and short-term illnesses (through certified and uncertified sick leaves), with an estimated 300 million working days lost at a cost of £55 million in social security benefit payments alone.

If an individual is affected, there must be repercussions for his or her family. Managers' wives, interviewed about moving, said of their husbands: "If he's happy, we're happy." (Marshall and Cooper, 1976). Conversely, if one family member (especially one as "powerful" as the head of the household) is showing symptoms of stress, this can seriously disrupt the whole pattern of family relationships. Seidenberg (1973) suggests that the stress thus caused helps to explain the recent rise (from 1:5 in 1962 to 1:2 in 1973) in the ratio of female to male alcoholics in the United States. A recent British study also depicts the wife as an indirect sufferer of stress effects. It concludes that the neglected wives of "workaholic" executive husbands turn for compensation to involvement in the unsatisfactory middle-class housing estates in which they find themselves.

For the country's employers of manpower, stress also has its costs: absenteeism being one of the more obvious. Stress-related illnesses are second and third in the table of those reasons for short-term sickness absence, which are on the increase in Britain (Office of Health Economics, 1971). Between 1954–1955 and 1967–1968 "nervousness, debility, and headaches" accounted for an increase of 189 percent of days off for men and 122 percent for women; "psychoneurosis and psychosis" of +153 percent for men and +302 percent for women. Still using "time off work" as our unit of measurement, we find that stress costs the economy substantially more than industrial injury (Taylor, 1974) and more than strikes (Gillespie, 1974). For example, in 1973 approximately 40 million days were lost to British industry because of "mental illness, stress, and headaches" (as accounted for by N.H.S. health certificates), which is three times the number of days lost by strikes and other forms of industrial action. There are other, less evident, costs of stress to the employer: high labor turnover rates, poor staff morale, and employees who do not find their jobs satisfying, which all increase an organization's costs while reducing its efficiency.

At a more macro level, American writers have tried to calculate the cost of stress to the national economy. They include in their accounts such items as loss of production, treatment, prevention, and the damage done by illegal behavior. Their estimates (for the mid-1960s) are, obviously, no more than gross approximations. They range from an annual cost of six to twenty billion dollars (McMurray, 1973 and Conley et al., 1973, respectively) or from 1 to 3 percent of the Gross National Product. Felton and Cole (1963) estimated that all cardiovascular diseases alone accounted for 12 percent of the time lost by the working population in the United States, for a total economic loss then of about $4 billion in a single year.

The commonly held belief about coronary heart disease, peptic ulcers, and other stress-related illnesses in terms of occupations and work is that they are found predominantly among professionals, that is, that they are the "bosses' diseases."

If we examine Table 3.1, we can see that frequencies of deaths in the U.K. due to major causes in the working population increase as we move from professional and white-collar jobs down to the unskilled. This applies both to stress-related illnesses such as ischaemic heart disease and to other illnesses such as pneumonia and prostate cancer. These statistics are very similar to mortality data from the United States and other developed countries. In terms of almost all the major and many of the minor causes of death among persons in the working population age groups, the blue-collar and unskilled are at greater risk than the white-collar and professional groups. This extends not only to mortality statistics but also to morbidity data as well. It can be seen in Table 3.2 that many blue-collar workers show a greater number of restricted activity days and consultations with general practitioners than do white-collar workers in the U.K. But does this mean that professional and managerial workers are not stress-prone, that their occupations and lifestyle minimize their vulnerability to stressors at work (and home) and, consequently, to minor and serious illness?

Cherry (1978), in a large-scale study on stress, anxiety, and work among 1,415 men, found that a higher proportion of professional and white-collar workers reported nervous strain at

TABLE 3.1 Deaths by Major Causes and Types of Occupations, 1970–1972 (Standardized Mortality Rates = 100)

Causes of Deaths, Persons Aged 15–64 (males)	Professional and similar	Intermediate	Skilled, nonmanual	Skilled, manual	Partly skilled	Unskilled
Trachea, bronchus, and lung cancer	53	68	84	118	123	143
Prostate cancer	91	89	99	115	106	115
Ischaemic heart disease	88	91	114	107	108	111
Other forms of heart disease	69	75	94	100	121	157
Cerebrovascular disease	80	86	98	106	111	136
Pneumonia	41	53	78	92	115	195
Bronchitis, emphysema, and asthma	36	51	82	113	128	188
Accidents other than motor vehicle	58	64	53	97	128	225
All causes	77	81	99	106	114	137

Source: U.K. Office of Population Censuses and Surveys.

TABLE 3.2 Acute Sickness and Consultations with General Medical Practitioners, 1974–1975

	Average Number of Restricted Activity Days Per Person Per Year (Males)			Average Number of Consultations Per Person Per Year (Males)		
	15–44	45–64	All ages	15–44	45–64	All ages
Professional	9	16	12	2.1	2.7	2.7
Employers and managers	11	13	14	1.8	2.4	2.7
Intermediate and junior nonmanual	10	21	15	2.0	4.3	3.1
Skilled manual and own account nonprofessional	15	24	17	2.8	4.0	3.2
Semiskilled manual and personal service	16	23	18	2.7	4.5	3.7
Unskilled, manual	21	28	20	3.5	4.8	3.6
All persons	13	21	16	2.4	3.8	3.1

Source: General Household Survey, 1974 and 1975 (by U.K. Government).

work than did skilled, semiskilled, and unskilled manual workers. Looking at her sample in terms of the U.K. Office of Population Censuses and Surveys categories, she found the following percentage of workers reporting nervous debility and strain at work: professional, 53.8 percent, intermediate non-manual, 56.9 percent, skilled (nonmanual), 44.3 percent, semiskilled (nonmanual), 50 percent, skilled (manual), 30.5 percent, semiskilled (manual), 15.3 percent, and unskilled (manual), 10.3 percent. This may only indicate that white-collar and professional groups differ from blue-collar occupations in their reactions to stress, that is, that the former reflect the pressures of work in mental illness, the latter in physical symptoms and illness. Although it may be true generally that there may be differences in stress manifestations between white- and blue-collar workers, there is certainly abundant evidence that there are even greater differences between the various occupations within both the white- and blue-collar categories. This was shown in a large-scale study carried out by a team of research workers at the Institute of Social Research at the University of Michigan (Caplan, Cobb, French, Van Harrison, and Pinneau, 1975). They carried out a study using self-report data in which they examined over 2,000 men employed in twenty-three occupational groupings from fork lift drivers, paced-assembly line operators, and electrical technicians to policemen, air traffic controllers, accountants, professors, and physicians. The primary purpose of their research was to try to identify differences between occupations in terms of their *sources* of stress, but if we examine a few of their crude measures of stress manifestations or illness we see that they found a variety of differences within blue-collar occupations and within white-collar occupations. For example, in blue-collar jobs, although they found a large number of self-reported illnesses or somatic complaints among machine-paced assembly workers, they found very few such complaints among continuous-flow workers; and in white-collar jobs, although they found a high incidence of somatic complaints among air traffic controllers, they found very few among professional engineers and computer programmers. They did, nevertheless, on an overall basis, find that the indices of ill health were greater for blue-collar workers than white-collar workers.

The value of the University of Michigan study was in identifying the sources of stress or stressors among the twenty-three different occupational groupings. In this respect there were two different groupings of stressors reported by blue- and white-collar workers respectively as responsible for job dissatisfaction and ill health. For the white-collar and professional workers, it was found that three major stressors differentiated them from blue-collar workers. They were *high and variable workload, responsibility for people,* and *job complexity and concentration.* For blue-collar workers, on the other hand, a different set of stressors were responsible for (ill) health related behaviors. They were *ambiguity about job future, underutilization of abilities, role ambiguity,* and *lack of job complexity.*

These research findings, in my view, highlight two important points about occupational well-being. First, if we examine in detail a variety of white-collar jobs it seems as if the primary precursors of stress and job dissatisfaction are a result of too little delegation and decentralization of tasks and decision making. On the other hand, many blue-collar workers (e.g., machine-paced assembly workers, machine tenders, etc.) seem to be suffering from quite the opposite stressors such as lack of job complexity, underutilization of skills and abilities, etc. This may indicate why there is a growing movement in Western Europe and North America for greater industrial democracy at work (e.g., autonomous work groups, group decision making, job redesign, etc.). It may be that greater movement in the direction of delegating decision making downward in a wide variety of jobs would not only alleviate stress among many of the white-collar and professional workers, but also encourage greater utilization of abilities and enhance job satisfaction among blue-collar workers. The results of the University of Michigan study, therefore, may help us on a global basis to understand the current trends and movements in the humanization of work, particularly job redesign and greater shop-floor participation in decision making. Second, the results from not only the Michigan study but many other studies as well (Cooper and Payne, 1978) indicate that to reduce job stress and maximize job satisfaction we must engage in an extensive *stress audit* of particular jobs. Building on the medical model, we must begin to carry out careful and detailed diagnoses of all aspects of a particular job, highlighting both its stress debits and credits. On the basis of this audit we can then begin to plan job and organizational change programs, in conjunction, of course, with the particular workers involved.

COPING
WITH PERSONAL
AND FAMILY STRESS
part II

Managing Your Type-A Coronary-Prone Behavior
chapter 4

Although a great deal has been written recently about the pressures and strains of worklife, identifying the sources of both professional, managerial, and shopfloor stress, little has been done to help people cope. As discussed earlier, Friedman and Rosenman showed a significant relationship between behavioral patterns of people and their prevalence to stress-related illness, particularly coronary heart disease (which now accounts for 41 percent of all deaths in males between the ages of 25 to 44!). They referred to this coronary-prone pattern as Type-A behavior or "hurry sickness." It is characterized by a style of living which includes "extremes of competitiveness, striving for achievement, aggressiveness, haste, impatience, restlessness, hyperalertness, explosiveness of speech, tenseness of facial muscles, and feelings of being under pressure of time and under the challenge of responsibility." On the basis of large-scale prospective epidemiological research they found that this behavioral pattern in *all* groups of people (e.g., executives as well as car assembly workers) was a significant precursor to coronary heart disease and other illnesses; indeed, they have found a six and one-half times greater probability of heart disease in Type As than their opposite number, which they refer to as Type Bs. Friedman and Rosenman don't claim that we should get rid of Type-A behavior, but rather that we should *manage* it; indeed, one might claim that in countries like Britain they should be encouraging Type A-behavior! From my work on British managers (Marshall and Cooper, 1979) it was found, ironically, that the most successful and satisfied executives are the classic Type As. Nevertheless, Type-A behavior can kill, so we must begin to manage and cope with it appropriately. Rather than advocate the systematic elimination of all sources of life and work stress, which may inadvertently have negative as well as positive consequences, I would like to suggest a number of coping strategies that any individual may find helpful to minimize the strains of contemporary existence.

Before we go into the various techniques and methods for managing your "hurry sickness" it might be useful for you, in the first instance, to assess your own Type-A behavior. On page 69, you will see a fairly simple questionnaire (based on work by Bortner and Rosenman, 1967) which will give you a rough idea of the extent of your Type-A behavior, as well as the particular behaviors that go to make up your "hurry sickness." There are obviously more detailed and sophisticated measures that have been used to assess this type of behavior, but this one should give you some crude measure of your own behavioral pattern. A number of scales are in reverse order, so that a high score on Type A-ness would reflect itself on the right-hand side of the continuum. This is to minimize "acquiescence response set," a psychological phenomenon in which some respondents agree with all statements (or only use one half of a particular scale) regardless of the content of the items. In this case, a high Type-A score is obtained on items 2, 5, 7, 11, 13, and 14 when circling the numbers on the right-hand side of the scale and for items 1, 3, 4, 6, 8, 9, 10, and 12 on the left-hand side. To score

YOUR TYPE-A BEHAVIOR

Please circle the number which you feel most closely represents your own behavior.

Never late	5	4	3	2	1	0	1	2	3	4	5	Casual about appointments
Not competitive	5	4	3	2	1	0	1	2	3	4	5	Very competitive
Anticipates what others are going to say (nods, interrupts, finishes for them)	5	4	3	2	1	0	1	2	3	4	5	Good listener
Always rushed	5	4	3	2	1	0	1	2	3	4	5	Never feels rushed (even under pressure)
Can wait patiently	5	4	3	2	1	0	1	2	3	4	5	Impatient while waiting
Goes all out	5	4	3	2	1	0	1	2	3	4	5	Casual
Takes things one at a time	5	4	3	2	1	0	1	2	3	4	5	Tries to do many things at once; thinks what he is about to do next
Emphatic in speech (may pound desk)	5	4	3	2	1	0	1	2	3	4	5	Slow, deliberate talker
Wants good job recognized by others	5	4	3	2	1	0	1	2	3	4	5	Cares about satisfying himself no matter *what others* may think
Fast (eating, walking, etc.)	5	4	3	2	1	0	1	2	3	4	5	Slow doing things
Easy going	5	4	3	2	1	0	1	2	3	4	5	Hard driving
Hides feelings	5	4	3	2	1	0	1	2	3	4	5	Expresses feelings
Many outside interests	5	4	3	2	1	0	1	2	3	4	5	Few interests outside work
Satisfied with job	5	4	3	2	1	0	1	2	3	4	5	Ambitious

the questionnaire, for items 1, 3, 4, 6, 8, 9, 10, and 12 give your-self a score of 10 if you circled the number 5 on the left-hand side, 9 for number 4, and so on with 0 if you circled number 5 on the right-hand side. Calculate in the opposite way for the re-maining items (2, 5, 7, 11, 13, and 14), that is, 0 for number 5 in the left-hand side, 1 for number 4, and so on until number 5 on the right-hand side which is scored 10. Then add up all the items for a total score, with a minimum of 0 and a maximum of 140 possible. The higher the score the greater your Type-A behavior. An examination of the individual items will indicate the particu-lar types of Type-A behavior you engage in. An awareness of the degree of "hurry sickness" (as Friedman and Rosenman term it), and of the particular behaviors involved should be the first step to changing or managing your "internal stress."

For those of you with substantial Type-A behavior prob-lems, we will attempt to provide you with suggestions about coping strategies you may want to try out.

Changing Your Type-A Behavior

First, you can begin to take the advice of people concerned with stress reduction, and there is no shortage of prescriptive suggestions here. By far, Friedman and Rosenman (1974) stand out as the most helpful if not the most unconventional. They recommend a number of "drills against hurry sickness," which they claim work for their Type-A patients. We will consider some of their suggestions from their book, *Type A Behavior and Your Heart.*

1. Try to restrain yourself from being the center of attention by constantly talking. Force yourself to listen to other people. "Begin in your avocational hours to listen quietly to the conversation of other people. Quit trying to finish their sen-tences. An even better sort of drill for you if you have been in the habit of hastening the other person's speech rhythms is to seek out a person who stutters and then deliberately remain tranquil."

2. If you continue to need to talk, even when there is no real need to do so, perhaps you ought to ask yourself the following questions: (1) "Do I really have anything important to say? (2) Does anyone want to hear it? and (3) Is this the time to say it? If the answer to any of these three questions is *no,* then remain quiet even if you find yourself biting your lips in frustration."

3. Try to control your obsessional time-directed life by making yourself aware of it and changing the established pattern of behavior. For example, "Whenever you catch yourself speeding up your car in order to get through a yellow light at an intersection, penalize yourself by immediately turning to the right at the next corner. Circle the block and approach the same corner and signal light again. After such penalization you may find yourself racing a yellow light a second, but probably not a third time." You can help yourself in social situations as well; indeed, you can seek out opportunities of controlling your Type-A behavior in almost all aspects of your life. "Purposely, with a companion, frequent restaurants and theaters where you know there will be a period of waiting. If your companion happens to be your wife, remember that you spend far longer periods of time alone with her in your own home without fidgeting. If you and your companion cannot find enough to say to each other as you wait in a restaurant or a theater, then you had both better seek different companions."

4. In order to put some of your Type-A behavior into perspective, it is important to carry out a number of exercises. Develop reflective periods in your self-created "hectic program for life," opportunities to assess the causes of your "hurry sickness." Perhaps one of the most important new habits you can establish is to review at least once a week the original causes of your present "hurry sickness." In other words, try to get to the source of your problems and current obsessions, to the reasons for your time-dominated behavior. Is it a need to feel important? Is it designed to avoid some activity or person? Is it really

essential to the success of a particular personal or organizational goal?" In respect to this latter point, follow Friedman and Rosenman's suggestion: "Never forget when confronted by any task, to ask yourself the following questions: (1) Will this matter have importance five years from now? and (2) Must I do this right now, or do I have enough time to think about the best way to accomplish it?"

5. Following on from the latter point, try to understand that the majority of your work and social life do not really require "immediate action," rather they require a quality end product or fulfilling relationship. So "tell yourself at least once a day that no enterprise ever failed because it was executed too slowly, too well. Ask yourself, Are good judgment and correct decisions best formulated under unhurried circumstances or under deadline pressures?"

6. In an effort to broaden yourself and lessen specific points of obsessional time-oriented behavior, it would be useful to indulge in outside activities; theater, reading, etc. For example, Friedman and Rosenman recommend to their patients that "for drill purposes, attempt to read books that demand not only your entire attention but also a certain amount of patience. We have repeatedly advised our Type-A patients to attempt reading Proust's seven volume novel *The Remembrance of Things Past* not because it is one of the great modern classics (which it is), but because the author needs several chapters to describe an event that most Type-A subjects would have handled in a sentence or two." In addition, if you want to get a clear picture of a person under stress, don't fail to read Joseph Heller's *Something Happened,* as mentioned earlier. It may help you to understand various facets of your own behavior as well as provide you with time to yourself.

7. Try not to make unnecessary appointments and unachievable deadlines. "Remember, the more unnecessary deadlines you make for yourself the worse your 'hurry sickness' becomes."

8. In addition, protect your time, learn to say *no.* "Try never to forget that if you fail to protect your allotment of time, no one else will. And the older you become, the more important this truth is."

9. Take as many stress-free "breathing spaces" during the course of an intensive work day as is possible. "Learn to interrupt long or even short sessions of any type of activity that you know or suspect may induce tension and stress before it is finished. Such stress is particularly apt to arise in the course of writing long memos, reports, or articles." Make sure you do something that relaxes you, it can mean reading a daily newspaper, taking a walk, talking to people you like, etc. The only constraint is that whatever you do it must take the pressure off your immediate task.

10. Try to create opportunities during the day or night when you can entirely relax your body and mind. Yoga has recently enjoyed popularity because it provides people with a technique to do this very thing. We shall be exploring this technique later in the book.

In addition to being concerned with time deadlines and commitments, most Type As are competitive and aggressive in their social and business relationships. This is demonstrated most aptly when one Type-A person meets another, as Friedman and Rosenman illustrate: ". . . if, on meeting another severely afflicted Type A person, instead of feeling compassion for his affliction you find yourself compelled to "challenge" him. This is a telltale trait because no one arouses the aggressive and/or hostile feelings of one Type A subject more quickly than another Type A subject." This is obviously due to a Type A's need to achieve and his impatience at reaching his goals (which, of course, he will never reach, because he continuously creates new ones). In addition, this aggressiveness partly stems from an inner self-insecurity and of his current position and status. All of this leads to frequent hostile and/or rejecting behaviors in his interpersonal relationships. In this context, Rosenman and Friedman attempt to suggest further methods of dealing with this aspect of Type-A behavior.

1. First, try to make yourself aware of your own behavior and its impact on other people. "If you are overly hostile, certainly the most important drill measure you should adopt is that one in which you remind yourself of the fact that you are hostile."

2. Not only should you minimize your hostility but also you should try to reward people for their efforts. "Begin to speak your thanks or appreciation to others when they have performed services for you. And do not do so, like so many hostile Type A subjects, with merely a grunt of thanks." This type of behavior may seem unnatural but it may help reestablish a different configuration of behaviors and extinguish the well-rehearsed hostile pattern. Associated with these kinds of behaviors is a generally more relaxed and positive approach to all relationships, e.g., greeting people more regularly, taking time off to develop social relationships, etc.

3. It is also quite frequently the case that Type As blame other people for not meeting their ideals or finding fault in others for their own failures or disappointments. "Over and over again, we have listened to Type As rationalize their hostility as stemming from their disappointment over the lack of ideals in their friends. We always have advised such sick people that they should cease trying to be 'idealists' because they are in fact only looking for excuses to be disappointed and hence hostile toward others."

These recommendations and many others by Friedman and Rosenman may seem unorthodox, almost absurd, but they are an attempt to modify internalized behavior patterns which have been established for many years, and which require unique and creative tactics and approaches.

A second orientation is to acknowledge the existence of your Type-A behavior and to try to live comfortably with it. This would necessitate a "do-it-yourself stress reduction" strategy, one which would encourage the individual to become aware of his/her symptoms of stress—physiological (e.g., stomach pains) or behavioral (e.g., aggressiveness, irritability)—and to take remedial action. This action may take the form of taking time off work, switching work activities, seeking professional help from the increasing army of personal counselors, or from outside sources, meditation, etc.

Meditation

Transcendental Meditation (TM), for example, has been reported to help work adjustment through the reduction of tension. Meditation involves concentration on a single stimulus which is repeated twice a day for approximately 20 minutes. The object of this technique is to restrict one's mental and physical states—the end result being a tranquil mind-body state. The effects of anxiety are kept to a minimum during this period of sustained concentration on a solitary object or word. A number of researchers have found that TM can subsequently improve performance, reduce short-term anxiety reactions, and increase span of attention. It has been argued by some psychologists that TM is most effective in breaking the threat-arousal-threat spiral, so that after the individual has experienced a stressful event he can relax himself.

The research evidence on the positive effects of TM is growing by leaps and bounds. In a review of the research in the sixties and up to the mid-seventies, Kuna (1975) suggested that the overwhelming research work supported TM as "an effective personal strategy for handling stress." His evaluation of the evidence indicated that TM had an efficacious effect on lowering anxiety, immunizing people to withstand stress, increased job satisfaction, and improved work performance. Dillbeck (1977) found that TM had a direct positive effect on anxiety level on thirty-three young anxious subjects. The subjects were divided into two groups, one learned TM for two weeks and the other just sat during their sessions for two weeks. The anxiety levels (psychometrically measured) dropped for the TM but not for the sitting group. A similar larger scale study was carried out by Puryear et al. (1976) with 159 meditators and controls. They found that anxiety scores on the 16PF and Mooney Problem Check List were significantly lower after meditation than for the controls. A number of studies on anxiety seem to show the same results—that TM has some effect on levels of nervous tension, although one is not quite sure how long the process lasts.

The more definitive research on TM shows that it has a more positive and longer lasting effect on some of our physiological processes, for example, raised blood pressure. In controlled studies by Benson et al. (Benson, 1973; 1974) it was found that there were substantial blood pressure decreases in hypertensive subjects. The control period of 6 weeks showed a 150 mm Hg av. systolic pressure. After three weeks of practice with TM the av. pressure was 142, after six weeks 140, and after nine weeks 135. A similar result was found in a study by Blackwell et al. (1976) among British hypertensives, with both short- and long-term improvements in a number of patients. Patel (1975) even found longer term effects among twenty experimental and twenty control subjects. The first group received three months' training in relaxation and meditation methods. In the next nine months they followed the described routine with a one month pause in between. After the first three months' training, the average systolic blood pressure in the trained group dropped by 20.4 mm Hg. and the diastolic blood pressure by 14.2 mm Hg. Twelve of the patients had reduced their medical treatment for high blood pressure by between 33 to 100 percent, but there was no marked change in the control group of patients. This effect persisted into the post-treatment period.

Although TM is increasingly being used in the treatment of hypertension and anxiety, there are those who contend it also has positive biochemical effects directly linked to stress-related illness (Michaels et al., 1976). This research is in its infancy, however, and more data is needed to confirm this trend. Nevertheless, TM and other relaxation techniques can in the short term help the individual to prepare his bodily processes for the stresses and pressures of everyday life.

Aside from the traditional TM which restricts awareness to concentrate on one single source or *mantra,* an activity which is usually repeated twice a day for approximately 20 minutes, one can use a whole range of relaxation techniques. For example, Peters and Benson (1979) suggest the following technique:

1. Sit quietly in a comfortable position.
2. Close your eyes.
3. Beginning at your feet and progressing up to your face, deeply relax your muscles. Keep them relaxed.
4. Breathe through your nose. Become aware of your breathing. As you breathe out, say the word *one* silently to yourself. Continue the pattern; breathe in . . . out, *one;* in . . . out, *one;* and so on. Breathe easily and naturally.
5. Continue for ten to twenty minutes. You may open your eyes to check the time, but do not use an alarm. When you finish, sit quietly for several minutes, first with your eyes closed and later with your eyes opened. Do not stand up for a few minutes.
6. Do not worry about whether you are successful in achieving a deep level of relaxation. Maintain a passive attitude and permit relaxation to occur at its own pace. When distracting thoughts occur, try to ignore them by not dwelling on them and return to repeating *one.* With practice, the response should come with little effort. Practice the technique once or twice daily but not within two hours of any meal, since the digestive processes seem to interfere with eliciting the relaxation response.

Edmund Jacobson (1958) has suggested an approach to stress relaxation which is different from the traditional approaches. He combines both psychological awareness of sources of stress with physiological manifestations and treatment. His approach of *progressive relaxation* consists of three stages: (1) trying to get the individual to focus on the causes or sources or situations that create the stress and tension, (2) the particular muscle reactions under these conditions, and (3) the continuous practice of muscle relaxation techniques to control this reaction. Brown (1977) in her book, *Stress and the Art of Biofeedback*, describes Jacobson's techniques in detail:

> Since a person generally has very little awareness of the *sensation* of relaxation, he is asked first to tense a set of muscles as hard as he can until he can feel real tension, even tenderness and pain in the muscles. Then he allows those muscles to relax, and tries to become aware of, to feel internally, the difference between tension and relaxation. For example, in some of the first exercises in Progressive Relaxation the patient is asked to hyperextend the wrist, i.e., to bend the hand so the back of the hand is aiming toward the top of the forearm. The muscles contracting the hand backward are tensed as much as the patient can, and are held until he feels the sensations of tension and even tenderness in the muscles of the upper side and about the middle of the forearm. Then the hand is flopped down to a loose, relaxed position. As a single exercise, this alternation between tensing and relaxing is practiced no more than about three times in a fifteen-minute period. A good share of the time is spent in trying to discriminate the feelings of tension and relaxation, i.e., the absence of tension. As practicing continues, the patient begins to discriminate more and more finely different degrees of tension and relaxation. The procedure is not hurried; each exercise with *each* set of muscles is practiced for perhaps two weeks, and only then does work begin with another set of muscles. Since the procedure goes progressively through all of the muscles in the body (hence its name), to accomplish the entire procedure requires considerable time, let alone persistence.

Then there is a whole set of relaxation techniques developed by Dr. Cary McCarthy:

Mental Relaxation (5-10 minutes)

1. Select a comfortable sitting or reclining position.
2. Close your eyes and think about a place that you have been before that represents your ideal place for physical and mental relaxation. (It should be a quiet environment, perhaps the seashore, the mountains, or even your own back yard. If you can't think of an ideal relaxation place, then create one in your mind.)
3. Now imagine that you are actually in your ideal relaxation place. Imagine that you are seeing all the colors, hearing the sounds, smelling the aromas. Just lie back, and enjoy your soothing, rejuvenating environment.
4. Feel the peacefulness, the calmness, and imagine your whole body and mind being renewed and refreshed.
5. After five to ten minutes, slowly open your eyes and stretch. You have the realization that you may instantly return to your relaxation place whenever you desire, and experience a peacefulness and calmness in body and mind.

Relaxation of Various Parts of Your Body (20 minutes)

1. Select a comfortable place to lie down. Remove shoes, loosen belt or light clothing. Stretch out on your back, arms resting by your sides, feet slightly apart, eyes gently closed.
2. Think to yourself, "I am now going to relax completely. When I waken I will feel fully refreshed."
3. Think about your feet, wiggle your toes, flex your ankles. Then "let go"—let go of all the tension, and let your feet rest limp and heavy.

4. Think of the lower part of your legs, your knees and thighs, up to your hips. Imagine them just sinking into the floor, heavy and relaxed.

5. Now think of your hands. Wiggle your fingers and flex your wrists, then let go, relax.

6. Think of your lower arm, elbow, and upper arm, all the way up to your shoulders. Picture all the tension just melting away.

7. Think about your abdomen. Let the tension go, and allow your breathing to flow more smoothly and deeply.

8. Think about your stomach and chest, up to your throat and neck. As you continue breathing more deeply, just imagine all the tension flowing out and you are relaxing more and more.

9. Now think about your throat, neck, and head, feeling limp and relaxed. Relax your facial muscles. Drop the jaw, parting the lips and teeth. Picture yourself completely relaxed.

10. If you are aware of any remaining tension anywhere in the body, go to the area mentally and relax the tension.

11. Continue to remain in this completely relaxed state for five to ten minutes. You may picture pleasant thoughts, or simply blank your mind and enter a stage of light sleep.

12. When you are ready to awaken, say to yourself, "I have been deeply relaxed. I am now ready to wake up, feeling completely refreshed and relaxed."

13. Begin to wake up by flexing the ankles, wiggling the toes. Then wiggle the fingers, and gently shake your wrists.

14. Bend the right knee, and then the left knee. Bend the right arm, then the left arm.

15. Open your eyes. Stretch each arm over your head. Then slowly sit up, stand up, and stretch again. You are ready to continue with your activities.

Number Count Down (3–10 minutes)

1. Select a comfortable position.

2. Close your eyes, and breathe deeply and rhythmically several times.

3. Take another deep breath, and while exhaling mentally visualize the number three (3). "3" is your symbol for complete body relaxation. (Relax any tension in your body, remembering the state of deep relaxation felt after the tensing muscle exercise.) Mentally repeat to yourself, "3, complete body relaxation."

4. Take another deep breath, and while exhaling mentally visualize the number two (2). "2" is your symbol for complete brain and nervous system relaxation. (Any thoughts, fears, concerns, worries—let them all go. Relax all thought processes, feeling a sense of mental stillness and harmony.) Mentally repeat to yourself, "2, complete brain and nervous system relaxation."

5. Take another deep breath, and while exhaling mentally visualize the number one (1). "1" is your symbol for complete Oneness within yourself, complete mind-body attunement and harmony. Mentally repeat to yourself, "1, Oneness, mind-body harmony."

6. In this deep state of mind-body relaxation, you are filled with calmness, peacefulness. You are one with the creative forces of your own being, and you may direct these creative forces to bring about positive changes and benefits in your daily life and health. (At this time give yourself positive health suggestions you wish to hear. If there is a particular part of your body that needs healing, imagine that your own health energies are flowing to that part. Create a tingling sensation, and imagine the body area bathed in pure light energy, restoring and renewing every cell and tissue.)

7. When you are ready to continue with your daily activities, say to yourself, "I have been in a deep, renewing state of mind-body relaxation. I will maintain the perfect attunement I have experienced, and will be in perfect health, feeling better than ever before. I will count from one to five, and at the count of five I will feel wide awake and in perfect health."

8. Then begin counting, "1 . . . 2 . . . 3 . . . 4 . . . 5." Open your eyes and say out loud (or repeat mentally with your eyes open), "I am wide awake, in perfect health, feeling better than ever before."

Most of these exercises can be found in Brown's (1977) excellent book *Stress and the Art of Biofeedback.*

Other Type-A Stress Management Techniques

Other techniques involve making the individual aware of his body's reaction to stress, whether it be physiological or psychological. Two techniques have been found to help individuals with stressful behavior to reduce their life stress—through "anxiety management training" and "visuo-motor behavior rehearsal." The individual learns the cues which signal the onset of stress, such as tightening of the muscles or increase in heart rate, and he is then taught to reduce this stress through training in muscle relaxation. This has been reported by Suinn (1976) to be effective in lowering stress in people faced with a variety of different personal and occupational problems.

A similar technique, using yoga and biofeedback, has been used with reasonable success in a preliminary study by Patel (1975). Individuals were taught how to relax and meditate while having continuous information about their progress from a biofeedback instrument, which served to reinforce their responses.

Another of the most interesting tools available for stress management is behavior modification. Suinn (1976) carried out a behavior modification program for Type As who had cardiac problems and were noticeably under stress. Type As were put through an experiential-based cardiac stress management training program designed to change their Type-A behavioral pattern of excessive deadlines, obsessional drives, etc. It consisted of a variety of relaxation exercises discussed above (e.g., meditation, deep breathing, etc.); desensitization or the retraining of reactions to stressful situations; reeducating the individual to control his environment by more sensibly allocating his time and managing the demands by people on his time; and finally by encouraging the individual to slow down all aspects of his "hurried" lifestyle. It was found after the program that most Type As had more control over their stress, had lower blood pressure levels and normal cholesterol counts, and they seemed to develop a style of living which was less hurried and more controlled. A review of the literature of behavior modification by Gavin (1977) seemed to indicate that this technique can have efficacious effects as a method of stress management for certain kinds of people and in certain situations.

Seeking
Social Support
chapter 5

A large number of studies have produced evidence indicating the importance of the social group to the individual as a source of job and life satisfaction (Cooper and Payne, 1978; 1980). For example, in terms of the work environment, the "human relations" approach to the workplace emphasized the role of social relationships in achieving satisfying and rewarding work (Cooper and Mumford, 1979). There is now substantial evidence that the individual's work group and social group may provide effective social support which can offset the effects of stress and coronary heart disease (Cooper and Marshall, 1978). One of the first indications of this appeared in several studies of social stress in Japan, which revealed marked differences in rates of coronary heart disease compared to the United States, which seemed to be related to certain features of Japanese lifestyle. In 1962 the ratio of death rate from coronary heart disease (CHD) to the total death rate was reported to be 33.2 for U.S. whites and 8.7 for the Japanese (Luisada, 1962). Matsumoto (1970) reported that two major factors seemed to be increasingly implicated in the development of CHD, namely high-fat diet and emotional stress. The diet hypothesis was strongly supported by the fact that the diet in Japan derives less than 16 percent of its calories from fat as compared to 40 percent in the American diet. Marmot and his colleagues at the University of California (Marmot et al., 1975) extended this work by looking at the differences between the two cultures in terms of social support and stress, controlling for high-fat diets. They studied 11,900 men of Japanese ancestry, aged between 45 to 69 (2,141 living in Japan, 8,006 in Hawaii, and 1,844 in California). It was found that age-adjusted prevalence of CHD increased from Japan to Hawaii, and again from Hawaii to California, where it is approximately double the rate in Japan. This trend was the same regardless of the criteria of heart disease, e.g., EKG or subjective assessments of angina pectoris. The incidence of abnormal EKG per 1,000 of the population (age adjusted) was 5.3 in Japan, 6.2 in Hawaii, and 10.8 in California. The incidence of diagnosed angina pectoris was 11.2 per 1,000 of the population (age adjusted) in Japan, 14.3 in Hawaii and 25.3 in California. They found that the known risk factors of hypertension, serum cholesterol levels, and smoking were roughly the same in all three regions, so that these risk factors could not be used to explain the differential appearance of coronary heart disease the further one went toward mainland United States. The investigators concluded that the acculturation among the Japanese Americans, that is, the extent to which they have abandoned their traditional way of life and moved towards a mobile, nuclear family, may be responsible for the differences. Marmot and his colleagues suggested further that the more hectic, demanding pace of life in the United States, together with the lack of social supports, of the extended family and a more extensive community of friends, are the likely culprits.

Since these studies a large research effort has been devoted to assessing the effect of lack of social support and stress-related illness and life/work dissatisfaction.

One of the largest studies carried out in the field of social support was done by the University of Michigan's Institute for Social Research. In their major publication *Job Demands and Worker Health* (Caplan et al., 1975) they did a comparative study of 23 occupations and over 2,000 workers. *Social support* was measured in these studies by asking the men to rate how much they could rely on people (their boss, other people at work, and friends and relatives) to help them or listen to them. This was done on a series of four-point Likert type scales for each of the three groups of people above. Table 5.1 provides the results of the study in terms of social support, work stressors, and health at work. The table indicates the correlations between the three support measures and measures of stress, strain, and physiological state. In terms of social support, it can be seen that all three support measures tend to alleviate perceived stressors (responsibility for persons, role ambiguity, and underutilization of skills and abilities). They also reduce the perceived strains of dissatisfaction, depression, and anxiety. It is also interesting to note that when they examined the degree of *participation* employees experience at work, that is, the extent to which they are included in the decision-making process affecting their jobs (a currently topical issue throughout Europe today in the move toward *industrial democracy*), this also had the effect of decreasing some relevant work stressors as well as improving individual well-being (e.g., lessening depression, anxiety, and job dissatisfaction).

Even before achieving proficiency at work, social support systems are needed. Mansfield (1972), for example, explored the stressful effects of entering industry for the first time. He found that recent graduates who entered industry faced severe identity-crises during the early months at work, but that the other new recruits provided the individual with the social support he/she needed to cope with this stress. Obviously, the

TABLE 5.1 Correlations Between Four Measures of Support and Selected Measures of Stress, Strain, and Physiological Variables

	Support of Supervisor	Support of Colleagues	Support of Family, Etc.	Participation
Responsibility for persons	0.17	0.32	0.22	0.39
Role ambiguity	-0.25	-0.20	-0.08	-0.18
Underutilization of skills	-0.23	-0.33	0.11	-0.39
Dissatisfaction	-0.34	-0.35	-0.15	-0.36
Anxiety	-0.10	-0.24	-0.05	-0.08
Depression	-0.30	-0.36	-0.20	-0.17
Heart rate	0.00	0.13	0.04	0.07
Cholesterol	0.04	0.04	-0.04	0.03
Uric acid	-0.11	-0.01	-0.01	0.03

Source: R.D. Caplan, S. Cobb, J.R.P. French, R. Van Harrison, and S.R. Pinneau, *Job Demands and Worker Health* (Washington, D.C.: National Institute of Occupational Safety and Health, Department of Health).

process of befriending peers, particularly ones who face similar identity-stress, is a very adaptive way of coping with episodic or short-term stress. On the other end of the occupational continuum, Gore (1978) did research on how unemployed workers coped with their stress. She looked at fifty-four rural and forty-six urban blue-collar workers (with a mean age of 49 years), over five periods of time during two-and-one-half years (e.g., anticipation period before unemployment, termination period immediately after being fired, and then six months, one year, and two years after termination). The actual event of being fired was considered the stressor, as well as the number of weeks unemployed and negative changes in economic circumstances. Self-reported measures of perceived stress and current state of health were collected, as well as serum cholesterol. Social support was measured by a questionnaire comprised of support from wife, friends, relatives, and the accessibility of community activities. She found that among individuals who had lost their jobs and who lacked social support from family, friends, and community, there were significantly more signs of emotional and physical ill health than those supported. They had a significantly higher serum cholesterol count (CHD risk factor), were more *depressed,* reported more illnesses, and perceived economic deprivation.

Not only at work but in other circumstances the wife/ husband and family are a major source of support for the individual. They provide the problem-solving, listening, and *accepting* behaviors that are essential to alleviating the stress, although they may be unable to change the circumstance that created them. For example, Burke, Firth, and McGratten (1974) examined the compatibility of 190 husband-wife pairs and their impact on stress management. The husbands were either engineers or accountants. They found that the more compatible were the husbands and wives, the greater the likelihood that they would cope better with stress-related problems at work and the home.

Indeed, Eitinger and Strom (1973) found that close social

support among Norwegian prisoners of war in Nazi concentration camps was essential to their survival. In a follow-up study of survivors, they found that individuals who had been able to retain close ties with their family, friends, and religious or political groups survived more often and were better able to adjust to normal life when freed. And in a much larger scale study by Myers, Lindenthal, and Pepper (1975), they found that individuals who were more integrated in society (as measured by being married, having children, of higher socioeconomic status, etc.) were much better able to cope with a variety of negative life crises and were significantly healthier than those not as integrated.

It is obvious, therefore, that support from the "significant others" at home and work and from the institutions we participate in, are critical to our ability to withstand and cope with the pressures of living in Type-A society.

The Family as a Support System

One of the most useful approaches to understanding the family as a support system was outlined by Caplan (1976) in a recent book. He suggested that the family serves a number of different support roles for its individual members: (1) as a collector and disseminator of information about the world, (2) as a feedback guidance system, (3) as a source of ideology, (4) as a guide and mediator in problem-solving, (5) as a source of practical service and concrete aid, (6) as a haven for rest and recuperation, and (7) as a reference and control group.

As a collector and disseminator of information the family provides its members with a history of how to cope; of how people lived and worked; indeed, of how they dealt with the problems of human existence. This was done much better by the extended family than it is now, since there was a wider pool of experience available to help structure and guide members of the family in their dealings with the outside and personal-internal world.

Another useful role the family fulfills is that of providing its members with feedback on their behavior, ideas, and feelings. As Caplan suggests, one can see this in respect of what goes on during a typical family meal. For example, a member of the family may take the opportunity of a meal of sharing his/her experiences to the others, while the other members provide their own views of them, by interpreting the meaning of the action, or putting it in the context of family or societal values or by providing alternative interpretations in terms of other people's reactions, and so on. The family as a *mirror* of our own values and behaviors is a tremendous source of support and "reality testing" institution.

The family is also a source of ideology: "The family group is a major source of the belief systems, systems and codes of behavior that determine an individual's understanding of the nature and meaning of the universe" (Caplan, 1976, p. 23). This framework for life can aid the individual during dilemma periods in his life, it can provide the kind of structure that can help him/her make crucial career, moral, and personal decisions. It is not that the family can provide the "right answers," but rather that the individual can have a "wall to lean against," or a psychologically "soothing cup of tea" in a demanding, fast-moving, achievement-oriented society.

Problem-solving can also be helped by the family in more practical ways, by providing guidance and mediation. The family brings a rich source of views, knowledge, and skills that can aid any individual member "in need." It can furnish generations of experience and competing views, past successes, and failures. It can also provide more practical and concrete aid in times of crisis—financial help, help with children, technical aid (e.g., cleaning, repairing, etc.) and employment. As Payne (1980) points out, however, "Help of a technical kind (within a family) is easier to give, but doing too much for a person not only runs the risk of retribution for the helper and the person being helped but may entail loss of self-esteem for the latter too."

One of the most important and supportive roles the family can play is as a haven of rest and recuperation. The family can help to protect its members, to provide a sanctuary for failures and disappointments, in effect, a place where you are *accepted* regardless of how the outside world has reacted to you or of the consequences of your actions. As long as the family member identifies with it, his deposit of membership and repository of past successes will motivate the family to help him/her over most present difficulties.

And finally, the family also acts as a reference group for its individual members, that is, it has a set of codes and values which it expects its members to adhere to as reasonable guides to living. The family takes an interest in matters that are important to its principles and thus to its very existence as an institution. Since the family has a detailed understanding of the development of the identity of all its members, it can strongly influence its members during times of stress and vulnerability, and can therefore serve as a potentially powerful force for support and change.

Work Organization Support

Work organizations provide a wide variety of social support systems to their employees. Payne (1980) suggests a framework for looking at organizational support at work which explores both the official or formal support systems and the informal ones (where the individual is both a giver and receiver of support). He also breaks down the areas of "support need" in terms of cognitive, emotional, and behavioral. Organizations obviously provide material support to accomplish a given task of work. Some organizations *care* for their employees better than others, that is, design better working environments, more sophisticated

TABLE 5.2 Forms of Organizational Support

	Material	Social		
		Cognitive	Emotional	Behavioral
Formal organization (rules, regulations and specialists)	Providing: Money Tools People Good physical environment Inducements	Advice by experts: Doctors Counselors Consultants Superiors	Support provided by experts: Counselors Occupational health nurses Welfare officers Supervisors (rarely)	Take person off job or change job Find someone else to solve problem Give early retirement Take responsibility from person
		Person Is Largely a Recipient		
Informal organization (mutual expectations and self-help)	Loaning to each other: Money Tools People Space Space	Pooling problem-solving resources by widening information network which may include 'experts' known personally to group members	Support spontaneously marshalled by the group. If given is more likely to be felt as genuine by the recipient	Help person to do the job or do it for him while he recovers Share responsibility with person
		Person Is Both Giver and Receiver		

Source: R. Payne, "Organizational Stress and Social Support," in C.L. Cooper and R. Payne, *Current Concerns in Occupational Stress* (London: John Wiley & Sons, 1980).

and time-saving machinery, more support staff, etc. Industrial democracy schemes such as autonomous work groups and greater worker participation in the decision-making process at work are materially improving the quality of life and the social support networks in industry.

Participation at Work. Volvo, for example, is one of the most talked about worker participation projects in the world. By now, worker participation at Volvo is so complex and far-reaching it is no longer possible to make a simple statement about it. The Kalmar plant is the boldest experiment Volvo has launched. Ten percent was added to building costs to have an assembly plant built to accommodate the principles of worker participation.

In the metal pressing section, workers have differently colored uniforms depending on their job. Blue is for worker, yellow for supervisor, and green for quality controller. The workers rotate jobs and the quota is set by the planning department and the union. No overtime is paid for working overtime. Employees work until the quota is met and then they have free time. If they finish early employees can take a swim or sauna at the plant.

In the body finishing section, there are several lines of work, each with its own characteristics. In one line the workers follow the cars on the conveyor and do each job as the car progresses past various tool stations. On other lines the workers stand in place and the car passes by. Workers use a variety of job rotating schemes to assemble the car. Some lines have workers in uniform and others have workers in their own clothes; workers make their own decision in this regard.

In the truck frame assembly section, the work is done in small teams of eight or ten with all the parts and tools available to assemble a complete unit. Workers elect their own supervisors, who are paid a marginally higher wage and can be replaced by a vote of confidence at any time. Replacement workers are brought in by consent. The team trains the new workers and brings them up to standard production.

Volvo is an assembly operation on twenty-one sites with 650 subcontractors making the components. There is only about three hours' warehouse suuply on hand at any one time. The corporate level has special divisions to lend support and finance, if necessary, to the subcontractors to keep them profitable and up to standard. There is no policy of amalgamating the contractors into a vertical manufacturing system as has been followed in most other motor industries.

Flexitime is widely practiced in a variety of forms. Often two women will work out the workload and split the shifts into smaller units or alternate days. The same is true of husband and wife teams.

There seems to be a commitment to cooperation and fair play at Volvo which is required in worker participation experiments. An example of the "working together" that goes on in Swedish industry is the Four Goals agreed on by the Swedish Employers' Association and the unions in 1972—increased productivity, greater job satisfaction, better working environment, and job security.

Participation at work seems to provide the social support that inoculates people against stress; it's a kind of substitute family group (as Marmot suggested about the Japanese). As early as the early forties Coch and French (1948) explored the impact of greater involvement and participation at work, in a study of three degrees of participation in a sewing factory. They found the greater the participation the higher the productivity, the greater the job satisfaction, the lower the turnover, and the better the relationships between boss and subordinates. These findings were later supported by a field experiment in a footwear factory in Southern Norway, where greater participation led to significantly more favorable attitudes by workers toward management and more involvement in their job (French, Israel, and As, 1960). There are many other research examples of the effect of participation as a support system on work-related criteria measures, as Figure 5.1 summarizes.

The research more relevant to our interests here, however, is the recent work on lack of participation (and social support) at work and stress-related disease. In a study carried out by French and Caplan (1973) on NASA personnel, for example, it was found that people who reported greater opportunities for participation in decision making reported significantly greater job satisfaction ($r = .50$), lower job related feelings of threat ($r = .51$), and higher feelings of self-esteem ($r = .32$). Buck (1972) found that both managers and workers, who felt under pressure most, reported that the supervisors "always ruled with an iron hand and rarely tried out new ideas or allowed participation in decision making." In addition, mutual support groups among the staff were discouraged and frowned upon. Margolis et al. (1974) found that nonparticipation and the absence of support systems at work, among a national representative U.S. sample of over 1,400 workers, was the most consistent and significant predictor or indicator of strain and job-related stress. They found that nonparticipation was significantly related to the following health risk factors: overall poor physical health, escapist drinking, depressed mood, low self-esteem, low life satisfaction, low job satisfaction, low motivation to work, intention to leave job, and absenteeism from work.

What Organizations Have Failed to Do to Create Support Systems

If we return to Payne's model presented earlier we can see that work organizations have within their power the opportunity of providing cognitive, emotional, and behavioral support systems to their employees. But what is the reality? In many, they provide only nominal cognitive advice, usually on aspects of worklife that they feel are directly appropriate, e.g., safety. In some firms, although very much in the minority, they extend

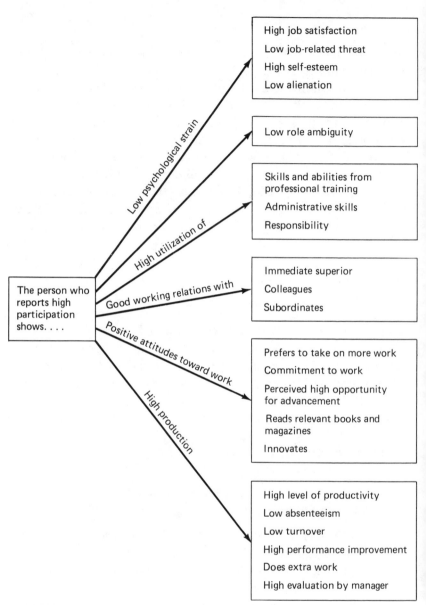

FIGURE 5.1 The Effect of Participation on Work-related Criteria Measures

Source: J.R.P. French and R. D. Caplan, "Organizational stress and individual strain," in ed. A.J. Marrow, *The Failure of Success* (New York: AMACOM, 1973), p. 52.

this to providing full fitness and health facilities for their employees. For example, Pepsico Inc. have provided a comprehensive physical fitness program at their world headquarters at Purchase, New York. They have a fully fitted gymnasium which includes sauna, an electrical treadmill, a striking bag, stationary bicycles, whirlpool, baths, showers, and massage facilities. In addition, they have a 1.15 mile running track which circles the HQ complex. This program is under the supervision of a full-time physical therapist and medical physician. Tailor-made exercise programs are planned for any interested employee by the physical therapist and doctor. Although this facility was originally planned for senior executives it is now used by all employees on a voluntary basis. The corporate headquarters are located in an attractive park-like setting to encourage an atmosphere of physical fitness. They also provide specialized programs such as aerobic dancing, weekly yoga sessions, and diet training to meet the needs of individual employees.

There is a clear-cut failure on the part of work organizations in the "emotional support" area. Very few private or public sector institutions provide the needed social support systems. When this does occur, it is the informal network at work that provides it. For a long time, work organizations felt that it wasn't within their scope of responsibility to provide counselors or psychiatric social workers or other sources of human support for their employees, particularly if the problem stemmed from the home environment, even if the problems at home may be affecting the person in the workplace. Indeed, it is increasingly difficult to draw a clear line between sources of stress that emanate from the family or work; the distinction is becoming less defensible. In addition, there are several other factors which are forcing organizations to take an interest in providing social support systems at work. One is the increasing litigation against companies for the stress that is alleged to be created in the workplace. The second is the increasing incidence of stress-like epidemics in factories and offices in many companies which has adversely affected absenteeism.

Cumulative Trauma. Cumulative trauma is a type of workers' compensation claim in which an employee contends that a major illness or disability is the cumulative result of minor job stresses and strains stretching back over a period of years. Any working person, be he a shopfloor worker in a car assembly plant or a corporation executive, if he is forced to give up work due to any type of illness (coronary heart disease, mental breakdown, nervous debility, etc.) can claim that this was due to the stress of his work over a period of years (i.e., cumulative). Since it is relatively easy to show that just about any job has a certain element of stress in it and since the law in various states (in particular, California, Michigan, etc.) allows a very liberal interpretation of stress-induced illness, the courts and appeal boards are accepting many of these claims. In addition, and even more importantly, the personnel executives and company medical directors are, in many cases, unable to provide the courts with evidence that they are trying to minimize the stresses and strains within the work environment. The years of neglect in regard to the well-being of staff in organizations has finally caught up with those responsible, and is forcing them to pay more attention and to provide more facilities in an effort at stress prevention at work.

For example, a man who was a well-paid sales director for a large company claimed and was awarded damages for cirrhosis of the liver, which he alleged was due to drinks that he had at business lunches with clients over a period of years. Another case was that of a man who was file clerk in a company for twenty years who ended up with arteriosclerosis (hardening of the arteries) and claimed (successfully) that this was due to the stresses associated with the sedentary "desk sitting" nature of his work. There are many other cases of successfully awarded disability damages due to cumulative trauma in the state of California.

Twenty percent of the workers' compensation claims that were paid in 1977 in California are expected to be cumulative trauma types, up from one percent in 1969. If we take a look at one of the largest industrial insurers in the state, Industrial Indemnity Company, we can see the extent of the problem. (See Table 5.3.)

In 1971, the insurance industry at large charged employers $3.7 billion in premiums for workers' compensation generally. Last year, due in large part to increased cumulative trauma claims, it rose to $6.1 billion. The law in California currently states that the liability for cumulative trauma can go back only five years, that is, the claimant can get compensation from all employers (and their insurance companies) during the last five years, with the exception that a person who is employed for a longer period with a single employer can claim back to the time when he contends he was first exposed to the health hazard. This severely penalizes the single employer, and since cumulative trauma wasn't anticipated by the employer or his insurance carrier ten or fifteen years ago (in terms of premium reserves), the claims are crippling them both.

Mass Psychogenic Illness. In addition to recent court decisions regarding cumulative trauma cases another aspect of stress at

TABLE 5.3 Industrial Indemnity Company, Cumulative Trauma (CT) Claim Results

Report Year	Initial CT Claim Reserves as Percentage of All New Indemnity Claim Reserves	CI Incurred Losses
1971	5.5	$2,270,000
1972	4.9	$2,587,000
1973	6.2	$3,848,000
1974	7.5	$5,560,000
1975	11.5	$8,045,000
1976	16.6	$10,925,000

work is worrying employers and health authorities. It is what the National Institute for Occupational Safety and Health term "mass psychogenic illness." They define it as "the collective occurrence of physical symptoms and related beliefs among two or more persons in the absence of an identifiable pathogen." In other words, it is a situation in which a number of workers in a particular plant or factory develop what appears to be some mysterious disease although there is no clearly identified micro-organism. The specific symptoms seem to vary from one industrial situation to another but they all consist of subjective somatic complaints, such as headaches, nausea, sleepiness, chills, etc. In all these cases, extensive biochemical and environmental tests (to check for harmful chemicals in the air) are carried out and nothing is found. There is, however, the presence of pre-cipitating psychosocial stressors in each of these work environ-ments. Most of these cases occur in industrial situations that involve repetitive tasks performed at fixed work stations and along paced assembly lines where there is excessive noise, poor lighting, and other discomforting environmental factors. In addition, they usually include workers who are engaged in "con-siderable unwanted overtime." In a large number of instances there is also poor industrial relations within the factory, as well as strained relationships between the shopfloor and first-line management in particular. Another curious facet of this situa-tion is that a large number of mass psychogenic incidents in-volve women workers. It has been suggested by the researchers for the U.S. National Institute for Occupational Safety and Health (Colligan and Murphy, 1979) that women may be more vulnerable to work stress of this kind because of the added difficulties of the conflicting demands of job and home as well as their tendency to externalize their emotions.

Several examples of this phenomenon were reported in a recent issue of the (U.S.) *Journal of Occupational Medicine,* from which one case example follows in full.

Background—The incident occurred in a frozen fish packing plant in the midwest. The plant employed approximately 168 workers on the first shift (116 females and 52 males).

Narrative—Thirty-three females and two males became ill approximately one hour after beginning work in the morning. Chief complaints were headaches, difficulty breathing, general weakness, and dizziness. Although unable to specify a probable cause, many of the affected workers had been involved in an incident of carbon monoxide exposure in the plant two years earlier. While admitting that the experienced symptoms were quite different on the two occasions, many of the workers nonetheless felt that the recent incident was a reoccurrence of carbon monoxide inhalation.

Findings—Biomedical testing of the affected workers and environmental sampling of the workplace failed to identify any toxicant capable of producing the observed symptoms. A continuous carbon monoxide monitor operating in the plant at the time of the incident indicated that CO levels were well below the recommended threshold limit value. Surveys and interview data indicated that, compared to a random sample of nonaffected workers, the affected workers (1) had more children at home; (2) had a lower personal income and worked less overtime; (3) were more dissatisfied with overtime pay; (4) were more dissatisfied with the amount of recognition they received from their supervisors and felt less able to influence their supervisors' decisions; (5) were more often affected by job layoffs; (6) would be more likely to quit their jobs if they didn't need the income; (7) perceived that the members of their work groups did not get along very well together; (8) reported their general health to be poorer; (9) more often felt tired at work and after work; (10) were more often bothered by noises and irritating odors; (11) actually witnessed more workers become ill; (12) perceived less peer cohesion and staff support within the environment; (13) perceived less personal freedom in the performance of their job; (14) perceived more production pressure; and, (15) scored higher on the extraversion dimension of the Eysenck scale. (Smith, Colligan, and Hurrell, 1978)

This case and the increasing number of similar incidents raises very dramatically the whole spectrum of the quality of life at work. Is the proverbial "absence due to flu" a possible case of stress contagion? Should those in industry look more systematically at these industrial epidemic-type illnesses (which we haven't done at the moment)? What can we do to create work environments which minimize the stress of work and its contagious effects? If we don't begin to answer these questions, increasing generations of young workers will live the reality of Studs Terkel's claim in his book *Working* that "work is...about violence to the spirit as well as the body. It is about ulcers as well as accidents, about shouting matches as well as fistfights, about nervous breakdowns as well as kicking the dog around. It is, above all . . . about daily humiliations."

Organizational Attempts at Improving Emotional Support. As a result of these two developments and a generally more humanistic approach to people at work, there are an increasing number of stress prevention programs oriented toward providing emotional support. For example, Kennecot Corporation have focused on the psychological health of their employees, providing extensive counseling facilities for all on-work and home-related problems. Indeed, they have even helped to organize alcoholic anonymous groups for employees and their families. Converse Corporation in Wilmington, Massachusetts did a variation on the emotional health approach by providing a voluntary relaxation program for their employees (Peters and Benson, 1979). Over 140 employees volunteered and were compared to 63 nonvolunteers who were selected randomly. The volunteers agreed to keep daily records for twelve weeks and to have their blood pressure measured. In addition, their general health and job performance were assessed during the experimental period. The results indicated that not only was a relaxation training break feasible within a normal work week, but that it led to general health, job performance, and well-being improvements, as well as significantly decreasing the blood pressure of employees from the beginning to the end of training.

Another even more adventurous emotion support program was carried out in the U.K. by Shell Chemical (U.K.). They set up a stress counseling program or what they termed an "employee counseling service" with a full-time employee counselor (with a psychiatric social work background). The goals of this facility are "to provide a confidential counseling service to all employees and their families," to work with outside helping professions for the welfare of employees, and other activities that enhance the quality of working life. After four years in operation, the counselor has been consulted by nearly 10 percent of the employees per annum. About half the employees who seek the service come for advice on education, family matters, work-related housing problems, divorce, separation, children, aged parents, and consumer affairs. The other half have developed a longer term case work or counseling relationship with the counselor on more fundamental individual, personal, or interpersonal problems. This is the kind of program that needs to be encouraged in industry and other types of organizations if we are to provide the emotional social support people need in the kind of modern society we all have created.

Informal Social Support at Work

One of the most important sources of social support is through the informal work group, as indicated by all the early Hawthorne studies and many others. For example, LaRocco and Jones (1978) did a large-scale study of 3,725 U.S. Navy personnel (enlisted men spanning the range of enlisted pay grades) on leader and coworker support and the stress-strain relationship. They concluded that support from boss and coworker were both positive and additive, that is, the more support one obtained from one's leader and coworkers the greater the lowering of the same manifestations of stress. This

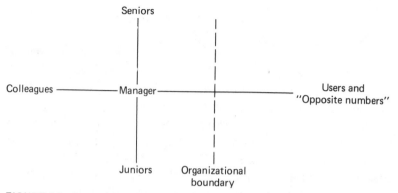

FIGURE 5.2 Cross of Relationships that Create Stress on Managers

Source: J. Morris, "Managerial stress and the 'cross of relationships,'" in eds. D. Gowler and K. Legge, *Managerial Stress* (Epping: Gower Press, 1975).

desire to seek the support of others in situations of danger or stress are not difficult to understand. As Wilson (1975) suggested in his concept of the "altruistic gene," man is genetically programmed to obtain security from the proximity of others because the larger the pack the fewer the animals that fall prey to predators.

The complicated set of relationships at work and their potential for conflict and ambiguity, as indicated for example by Morris (1975) in respect to managers in an organization, make it necessary for individuals to seek support from their peers. In this respect, there are a number of different approaches one can take. First, responsibility for people within organizations should create the right atmosphere to encourage social support networks as well as to provide the most appropriate resources for stress management. We will discuss this further in Chapter 8. Second, the individual can do something to help himself create these networks. Let us explore a number of steps an individual under stress may take to help himself at work (assuming there is no formal social support system available):

1. Pick somebody at work you feel you can talk to; someone you don't feel threatened by and to whom you can trustfully reveal your feelings to. Don't use people who, on reflection, you may be using on an unconscious level as a pawn in a game of organization politics!

2. Approach this person and explain to him/her that you have a particular problem at work or outside that you would like to discuss. Admit that you need help and that he or she would be the best person to consult because you trust his/her opinion, like him/her as a person, feel that you can usefully identify with your circumstance, etc.

3. Try to maintain and build on this relationship, even at times of no crisis or problems.

4. Review, from time to time, the nature of the relationship, to see if it is still providing you with the emotional support you need to cope with the difficulties that arise. If the relationship is no longer constructive or the nature of your problems has changed (requiring a different peer counselor), then seek another person/s for support.

It might be useful, however, to have some method of selecting this peer counselor. Fiedler (1967) has provided a useful questionnaire which might help in this regard, although it was not intended for this purpose. It is called the Most Preferred Coworker scale (see pages 106–07). First think of the person you feel would help you the most in coping with your work stress. He/she may be someone you work with now or someone you knew in the past. Describe this person as he appears to you by placing an X between the appropriate colons for each set of bipolar adjectives. After you have completed this for all the items, try to think of a person currently in your workplace who best fits this pattern of results.

This approach to social support at work may seem terribly contrived, but it is important for anyone of us in need of help to "own up" to our difficulties and not to rely totally on *the organization* to always be there to resolve them. We must take personal initiatives to seek the kind of professional or "peer"

MOST PREFERRED COWORKER SCALE

	Very	Quite	Somewhat	Slightly
Pleasant	:_____	:_____	:_____	:_____
	8	7	6	5
Friendly	:_____	:_____	:_____	:_____
	8	7	6	5
Rejecting	:_____	:_____	:_____	:_____
	1	2	3	4
Helpful	:_____	:_____	:_____	:_____
	8	7	6	5
Unenthusiastic	:_____	:_____	:_____	:_____
	1	2	3	4
Tense	:_____	:_____	:_____	:_____
	1	2	3	4
Distant	:_____	:_____	:_____	:_____
	1	2	3	4
Cold	:_____	:_____	:_____	:_____
	1	2	3	4
Cooperative	:_____	:_____	:_____	:_____
	8	7	6	5
Supportive	:_____	:_____	:_____	:_____
	8	7	6	5
Boring	:_____	:_____	:_____	:_____
	1	2	3	4
Quarrelsome	:_____	:_____	:_____	:_____
	1	2	3	4
Self-assured	:_____	:_____	:_____	:_____
	8	7	6	5
Efficient	:_____	:_____	:_____	:_____
	8	7	6	5
Gloomy	:_____	:_____	:_____	:_____
	1	2	3	4
Open	:_____	:_____	:_____	:_____
	8	7	6	5

Source: F.E. Fiedler, *A Theory of Leadership Effectiveness* (New York: McGraw-Hill, 1967).

Slightly	Somewhat	Quite	Very	
___ :	___ :	___ :	___ :	Unpleasant
4	3	2	1	
___ :	___ :	___ :	___ :	Unfriendly
4	3	2	1	
___ :	___ :	___ :	___ :	Accepting
5	6	7	8	
___ :	___ :	___ :	___ :	Frustrating
4	3	2	1	
___ :	___ :	___ :	___ :	Enthusiastic
5	6	7	8	
___ :	___ :	___ :	___ :	Relaxed
5	6	7	8	
___ :	___ :	___ :	___ :	Close
5	6	7	8	
___ :	___ :	___ :	___ :	Warm
5	6	7	8	
___ :	___ :	___ :	___ :	Uncooperative
4	3	2	1	
___ :	___ :	___ :	___ :	Hostile
4	3	2	1	
___ :	___ :	___ :	___ :	Interesting
5	6	7	8	
___ :	___ :	___ :	___ :	Harmonious
5	6	7	8	
___ :	___ :	___ :	___ :	Hesitant
4	3	2	1	
___ :	___ :	___ :	___ :	Inefficient
4	3	2	1	
___ :	___ :	___ :	___ :	Cheerful
5	6	7	8	
___ :	___ :	___ :	___ :	Guarded
4	3	2	1	

help that may be necessary if we experience the kind of pressure at work we feel we can't adequately cope with ourselves.

Conclusion

There are those who argue that individuals can survive and, indeed, thrive in Western organizations, if only the work environment provided the "social support" it does in Japan. As we discussed earlier, coronary heart disease in Japan is much lower than in most Western countries and there is now some evidence that the individual's work group and social group provide effective social support which offsets some of the effects of stress and coronary heart disease. Although many people in the West ridicule the structure of Japanese corporate life and the "Japanese organizational man," it is these very institutions (e.g., shared decision making, group affiliations, corporate identity, group counseling, etc.) that play an important role in decreasing the frequency of stress-related disease in Japan. As one of the leading researchers in 'this field has said: "The deleterious circumstances of life need not be expressed in malfunctioning of the physiologic or psychologic systems if a meaningful social group is available through which the individual can derive emotional support and understanding."

Reprogramming
Your Lifestyle
chapter 6

Bob Slocum, the protagonist in Heller's 1974 novel, *Something Happened,* poignantly surveyed his life and career as follows:

> I call these charts my Happiness Charts. . . . At the very top, of course, are those people, mostly young and without dependents, to whom the company is not yet an institution of any sacred merit (or even an institution especially worth preserving) but still only a place to work, and who regard their present association with it as something temporary. To them, it's all just a job, from president to porter, and pretty much the same job at that. I put these people at the top because if you asked any one of them if he would choose to spend the rest of his life working for the company, he would give a resounding *No!*, regardless of what inducements were offered. I was that high once. If you asked me that same question today, I would give you a resounding *No!* and add:

> 'I think I'd rather die now.'

> But I am making no plans to leave.

> I have the feeling now that there is no place left for me to go.

I found Heller's character depressing, because he seems trapped in a particular lifestyle that he finds neither satisfying nor meaningful. But even more disturbing is that he doesn't care, he makes no attempt to do anything about it. He sees life as inextricably "determined" and predictable. It is this attitude and approach to life that is responsible for a great deal of unhappiness, depression, anxiety, and in the long term, for stress-related illnesses (both physical and psychological).

We all have, to some degree, the opportunity to control our own destiny and change our lifestyle. It is unfortunate, however, that many people begin to realize this only when it is too late—when they are on the verge of death, for example, Tolstoy's Ivan Ilych acknowledged this as he awaited his end:

> "What if my whole life has been wrong?" It occurred to him that what had appeared perfectly impossible before, namely that he had not spent his life as he should have done, might after all be true. It occurred to him that his scarcely noticeable impulses which he had immediately suppressed, might have been the real thing, and the rest false. And his professional duties and the whole arrangement of his life and of his family, and all his social and official interests, might all have been false. He tried to defend all those things to himself and suddenly felt the weakness of what he was defending. There was nothing to defend. . . .

Dyer (1976), the author of *Your Erroneous Zones,* talks about *self-immobilization* as the force of resistance to change in one's particular life circumstance, which ranged from total inaction to mild indecision to hesitancy. He argues that one must attempt to cut through this unhealthy, yet understandable, process so that one can release what he terms our "potential for happiness." His approach is to try and get the individual to focus on those aspects of his lifestyle that may be creating immobility; for example, he suggests a number of possible behaviors that reflect these states:

"You are immobilized when . . .

You can't talk lovingly to your spouse and children though you want to.

You can't work on a project that interests you.

You don't make love and would like to.

You sit in the house all day and brood.

You don't play golf, tennis, or other enjoyable activities, because of a leftover gnawing feeling.

You can't introduce yourself to someone who appeals to you.

You avoid talking to someone when you realize that a simple gesture would improve your relationship.

You can't sleep because something is bothering you.

Your anger keeps you from thinking clearly.

You say something abusive to someone that you love.

Your face is twitching, or you are so nervous that you don't function in the way you would prefer."

Dyer's philosophy is very simple—an individual must be able to identify the problem areas, or internalized lifestyle patterns that are preventing him or her from achieving important life goals, and then "cut through the lifetime of emotional red tape" by changing behavior and redesigning these patterns. What one mustn't do—*and this is the cardinal rule*—is to blame *circumstance* or *somebody else* for failures or an unsatisfying mode of living. Individuals must "own up" and choose their own more appropriate lifestyle. George Bernard Shaw put it succinctly in his novel, *Mrs. Warren's Profession:* "People are always blaming their circumstances for what they are. I don't believe in circumstances. The people who get on in this world are the people who get up and look for the circumstances they want, and if they can't find them, make them."

Low Stress Lifestyle

There is no absence of "advice givers" when it comes to recommending alternative lifestyles. Psychologists, medics, and management gurus (not unlike myself!!) are readily available to provide the latest panaceas for "living creatively and healthily." Not that these suggestions are useless or uninspiring, but rather they tend to be fairly prescriptive. Nevertheless, they can be helpful to those who need some guidelines to what, at least, other people feel are "reasonable living patterns." Albrecht (1979), for example, provides a rich behavioral syndrome of a low stress lifestyle. As one can see, many of the elements of this lifestyle are common sense modes for living, while others provide more unique suggestions; for example, having "escape routes" that allow occasional detachments and relaxation and encourage individuals to spread their investments of energy in a variety of activities. In terms of this latter point it is interesting to reflect on what Charles Darwin said during the later stages of

TABLE 6.1 High and Low Stress Lifestyles

Stressful Lifestyle	*Low-stress Lifestyle*
Individual experiences chronic, unrelieved stress	Individual accepts "creative" stress for distinct periods of challenging activity
Becomes trapped in one or more continuing stressful situations	Has "escape routes" allowing occasional detachment and relaxation
Struggles with stressful interpersonal relationships (family, spouse, lover, boss, coworkers, etc.)	Asserts own rights and needs; negotiates low-stress relationships of mutual respect; selects friends carefully and establishes relationships that are nourishing and nontoxic
Engages in distasteful, dull, toxic, or otherwise unpleasant and unrewarding work	Engages in challenging, satisfying, worthwhile work that offers intrinsic rewards for accomplishment

TABLE 6.1 continued

Stressful Lifestyle	Low-stress Lifestyle
Experiences continual time stress; too much to be done in available time	Maintains a well-balanced and challenging workload; overloads and crises are balanced by "breather" periods
Worries about potentially unpleasant upcoming events	Balances threatening events with worthwhile goals and positive events to look forward to
Has poor health habits (e.g., eating, smoking, liquor, lack of exercise, poor level of physical fitness)	Maintains high level of physical fitness, eats well, uses alcohol and tobacco not at all or sparingly
Life activities are "lopsided" or unbalanced (e.g., preoccupied with one activity such as work, social activities, making money, solitude, or physical activities)	Life activities are balanced: individual invests energies in a variety of activities, which in the aggregate bring feelings of satisfaction (e.g., work, social activities, recreation, solitude, cultural pursuits, family and close relationships)
Finds it difficult to just "have a good time", relax, and enjoy momentary activities	Finds pleasure in simple activities, without feeling a need to justify playful behavior
Experiences sexual activities as unpleasant, unrewarding, or socially "programmed" (e.g., by manipulation, "one-upping")	Enjoys a full and exuberant sex life, with honest expression of sexual appetite
Sees life as a serious, difficult situation; little sense of humor	Enjoys life on the whole; can laugh at himself; has a well-developed and well-exercised sense of humor
Conforms to imprisoning, punishing social roles	Lives a relative role-free life; is able to express natural needs, desires, and feelings without apology
Accepts high-pressure or stressful situations, passively; suffers in silence	Acts assertively to reengineer pressure situations whenever possible; renegotiates impossible deadlines; avoids placing himself in unnecessary pressure situations; manages time effectively

Source: Karl Albrecht, *Stress and the Manager* (Englewood Cliffs, N.J.: Prentice-Hall, 1979), pp. 107–8.

his life: "My mind seems to have become a kind of *machine* for grinding general laws out of large collections of facts but why this should have caused the *atrophy* of that part of the brain alone on which the *higher tastes* depend, I cannot conceive. . . . The loss of these tastes is a loss of happiness and may possibly be injurious to the *intellectual* and more probably the *moral* character, by enfeebling the *emotional* part of our nature."

As well as focusing on the prescriptive strategies for living, one might be well advised to explore the various alternative lifestyles in terms of their processes and consequences. Once again, there are a host of theorists who can provide useful conceptual frameworks. One of the comparisons I have found helpful which focuses on some of the more relevant and topical behavioral lifestyles was posited by Steinmetz (1977).

As can be seen in the table, Dr. Steinmetz examines three main behavioral styles: passivity, assertiveness, and aggressiveness. This is explored from the perspective of how the individual feels about his particular predominant lifestyle and the effect it has on the individual and the significant others in his or her life. Her approach is not to provide prescriptive "guides to living," but to highlight the impact of particular approaches to relationships. So, for example, individuals who develop a predominantly *passive* stance in their relationships with other people tend to feel ignored, helpless, and undervalued, which creates reciprocally incompatible responses from others (e.g., frustration or guilt by domination). The ultimate outcome in this type of encounter is that other people tend to achieve their objectives in life at your expense or, alternatively, they feel that others are manipulating them (which becomes a self-fulfilling prophecy).

Life Planning

Probably a better approach to reprogramming your own stress lifestyle, assuming it is *not* providing you with what you need as a person, is to do some systematic "life planning." Pfeiffer and Jones in their books, *Structured Experiences for*

TABLE 6.2 Comparison of Alternative Behavior Styles

	Passive	Assertive	Aggressive
Characteristics	Allow other to choose for you. Emotionally dishonest. Indirect, self-denying, inhibited, Win-Lose Situation which you lose. If you do get your own way, it is indirect.	Choose for self. Appropriately honest. Direct, self-respecting, self-expressing, straightforward. Convert Win-Lose to Win-Win.	Choose for others. Inappropriately honest (tactless). Direct, self-enhancing. Self-expressive, derogatory. Win-Lose situation which you win.
Your own feelings on the exchange	Anxious, ignored, helpless, manipulated. Angry at self and/or other.	Confident, self-respecting, goal oriented, valued. Later: accomplished.	Righteous, superior, depreciatory, controlling. Later: possibly guilty.
Others' feelings in the exchange	Guilty or superior. Frustrated with you.	Valued, respected.	Humiliated, defensive, resentful, hurt.
Others' view of you in exchange	Lack of respect. Distrust. Can be considered a pushover. Do not know where you stand.	Respect, trust, know where you stand.	Vengeful, angry, distrust, fear.
Outcome	Others achieve their goals at your expense. Your rights violated.	Outcome determined by aboveboard negotiation. Yours and others rights respected.	You achieve your goal at other's expense. Your rights upheld; others violated.
Underlying belief system	I should never make anyone uncomfortable or displeased . . . except myself.	I have a responsibility to protect my own rights, and I respect others but not necessarily their behavior.	I have to put others down in order to protect myself.

Source: J. Steinmetz, "The stress reduction program at University Hospital, University of California Medical Center, San Diego," in *Proceedings of the Conference on Occupational Stress* held by UCLA and the N.I.O.S.H, November 1977.

Human Relations Training and *Handbook for Group Facilitators,* have provided a valuable service in providing individuals and professionals concerned with human relations with a compendia of exercises to aid in understanding interpersonal, group, and organizational behavior. In one of their early books they provided group facilitators with an interesting exercise on "life planning" which can be easily adapted for individual use (Pfeiffer and Jones, 1970, pp. 113-138).

There are three parts to this exercise. In the first part you are encouraged to find out "where I am now" in terms of your *career, personal life* (e.g., family and friends), and *personal fulfillment.* The first step in answering this question is to draw a graph or life line (something like a sales chart, which can be straight or curved) that depicts the past, present, and future of your *career.* On this line, mark an X to show where you are now. Then write a brief explanation of the *career line* you have drawn, highlighting the high points and the low points. This is not too dissimilar an approach from Bernard Bass' (1970) *Exercise Future,* which encourages an individual at work to explore his expectations and goals and its implications for career planning. Repeat the same procedure for your *personal life,* that is, draw a graph line which depicts the past, present, and future of your personal affiliations (family and friends), marking an X to indicate where you are now. Again, write a brief explanation of your *personal life line,* describing in detail your troughs and peaks. And finally, repeat the procedure one more time by drawing a *personal fulfillment line,* considering every level of your internal personal world, based on your past, present, and future behavior. Once again, mark an X on the line and then write a brief description of your high and low points.

This part of the exercise should give you some idea of where you've come from, where you are now, and where you are likely to go. In terms of your *future* career, personal life, and personal fulfillment, you may feel that they reflected either where you would *ideally* like to go or where you think you are likely to end up (although you would rather not). In either case, it should provide you with the kind of personal data you can use to plan future life activities so that you can better attain your objectives.

In the second part, the individual is encouraged to find out "who am I" by writing down on a piece of paper up to twenty adjectives which describe *you* most accurately in terms of your *career,* then twenty adjectives which best describe your *personal life* and *personal fulfillment.* After you have finished this procedure, regroup each of your lists separately into the following three categories: positive, neutral, and negative. This regrouping should provide you with an awareness of your positive and negative traits in three of the major aspects of your life—work, family, and personal.

In the third part, you are encouraged to find out "where do I want to be". Here you are asked to list up to ten *ideal attainments* in each of the three main areas of your life—*career, personal life,* and *personal fulfillment.* You are asked to be as free as possible, allowing yourself to fantasize on goals you wish you could achieve in each area. For example, "I want to become President of my company" may be a career ideal, or "I want to be able to really communicate with my teenage son" may be a personal life ideal, or "I want to learn to control my fear of heights" may be a personal fulfillment ideal. Then assign a priority value to the career ideals, personal life ideals, and personal fulfillment ideals, using the following scale: 4—of *very great importance,* 3—of *great importance,* 2—of *moderate importance,* and 1—of *little importance.* For the next stage, rerank all three goal lists (e.g., career, personal life, and personal fulfillment) together, with the items scoring 4 at the top, those scoring 3 next, and so on. This combined list should reflect the relative importance of specific goals regardless of whether they are career, personal, or family ones. This then provides you with information about your *ideal goal states* in life. If most of the goals rated 4 are in one particular life area, such as in the family, this will indicate the degree of importance you place in the family. On the other hand, you may find your 3 and 4 ratings widely scattered among all three areas but with certain under-lying trends such as the importance and value you place on, for example, "relationships with other people", whether they are at work, in the home, or in other areas of your life.

Whatever the configuration of your *ideal goal* list, the next thing to do is to begin some form of life planning. What you might do in this respect is to select, say, the first five goals from your list and establish a program to achieve them; this will probably entail a detailed series of stages with deadlines and well thought out behavioral, emotional, or practical strategies for their attainment. You may find this is easier to do if you were working with somebody else, that is, that you could share your goals and levels of attainment as you were progressing through your self-directed program. If this would be useful, deliberately try to seek some support from a trusted work col-league, friend, or family member. Your life planning program may, in any case, necessitate this kind of sharing or working together.

There are a wide variety of life planning techniques avail-able, but the one we have just gone through should provide you with the essence of the approach and how you can help yourself in trying to achieve more of your valued life goals. Nobody is saying that this is an easy approach; indeed, it requires a great deal of introspection, planning, and initiative. There are many people, however, who feel that the alteration of life plans and styles is best achieved by involving the potential changes in the process of change. As the old adage goes: "Spoonfeeding teaches you only the shape of the spoon."

Life Change and Stress

In addition to better understanding the nature of your life-style and goals in an effort to reduce its stresses and strains, it is also important to realize that the amount of change that is taking place in your life may be causing you irreparable harm. These can stem from factors beyond your control, such as the death of a close relative, and to some which you are party to (either wittingly or involuntarily), such as divorce, pregnancy, etc.

A considerable body of work along these lines in the last fifteen years had led to the suggestion that life change per se is a preconditioning factor in stress-related illness. Wyler, Holmes, and Masuda, a group of research workers at Washington University conducted a survey (Wyler, Masuda, and Holmes, 1971; Holmes and Masuda, 1973) from which they calculated the relative amounts of "social adjustment" required after certain life events. They were then able to apply these weightings to the events in the lives of selected sample populations, and to arrive at their "life change scores" for a given period. In their studies (which have been both retrospective and prospective), they found high life change scores to be related to the onset of illness within the following two-year period. Correlational studies suggest a relationship between life change score and the onset of tuberculosis, heart disease, skin disease, and hernia, a general deterioration in health and poorer academic performance (Holmes and Masuda, 1973). Wyler, Masuda, and Holmes (1975) also purport to show that the greater the life change experienced the more serious the disease that develops. Myers, Lindenthal, and Pepper (1971) also found a relationship between life events and psychiatric symptomatology in a community study in Connecticut. A net increase in life events was associated with worsening symptoms, a net decrease with improvement. These researchers contend that the nature of the change—whether it is favorable or unfavorable, competitive or complementary—is immaterial.

The global applicability of these findings has, however, been challenged, particularly on methodological issues. Brown, Sklair, Harris, and Birley (1973) and Mechanic (1974) provide extensive reviews of the many research problems. Acting on some of these criticisms, they and other researchers have made considerable refinements to the original techniques and have gone on to establish relationships between certain classes of life events and, for example, alcoholic relapse or the onset of schizophrenia. While the simplistic nature of Holmes and colleagues' early findings is now being questioned, their basic conclusion that there is a link between changes in life events and the onset of illness is generally accepted.

The following life stress inventory has been used extensively as a measure of life event change and susceptibility to stress-related ill health. Although the Scale can give you some indication of the probability of health breakdown given a large number of simultaneously occurring stressful events, it doesn't take into account a number of very important factors in the stress-strain equation. The extent to which these events do indeed lead to ill health will, of course, depend on your personal capacity to cope with stress, on the support systems you have in your environment (at work, home, etc.), on how important or significant that life event is to you personally (for although there are values assigned to each life event, they are *means* established on a large validating sample, so that for any one person his own value score might differ quite significantly from the mean value), and so on. It can give you some idea, however, of the extent of the change stressors you are experiencing in a variety of life areas, and alert you to the potential dangers or otherwise of your current situation.

THE HOLMES-RAHE LIFE STRESS INVENTORY

THE SOCIAL READJUSTMENT RATING SCALE

Instructions: Check off each of these life events that has happened to you during the previous year. Total the associated points. A score of 150 or less means a relatively low amount of life change and a low susceptibility to stress-induced health breakdown. A score of 150 to 300 points implies about a 50 percent chance of a major health breakdown in the next two years. A score above 300 raises the odds to about 80 percent, according to the Holmes-Rahe statistical prediction model.

LIFE EVENT	MEAN VALUE
1. Death of spouse	100
2. Divorce	73
3. Marital separation from mate	65
4. Detention in jail or other institution	63
5. Death of a close family member	63
6. Major personal injury or illness	53
7. Marriage	50
8. Being fired at work	47
9. Marital reconciliation with mate	45
10. Retirement from work	45
11. Major change in the health or behavior of a family member	44
12. Pregnancy	40
13. Sexual difficulties	39
14. Gaining a new family member (e.g., through birth, adoption, oldster moving in, etc.)	39
15. Major business readjustment (e.g., merger, reorganization, bankruptcy, etc.)	39
16. Major change in financial state (e.g., a lot worse off or a lot better off than usual)	38
17. Death of a close friend	37
18. Changing to a different line of work	36
19. Major change in the number of arguments with spouse (e.g., either a lot more or a lot less than usual regarding child-rearing, personal habits, etc.)	35
20. Taking on a mortgage greater than $10,000 (e.g., purchasing a home, business, etc.)	31

21.	Foreclosure on a mortgage or loan	30
22.	Major change in responsibilities at work (e.g., promotion, demotion, lateral transfer)	29
23.	Son or daughter leaving home (e.g., marriage, attending college, etc.)	29
24.	In-law troubles	29
25.	Outstanding personal achievement	28
26.	Wife beginning or ceasing work outside the home	26
27.	Beginning or ceasing formal schooling	26
28.	Major change in living conditions (e.g., building a new home, remodeling, deterioration of home or neighborhood)	25
29.	Revision of personal habits (dress, manners, associations, etc.)	24
30.	Troubles with the boss	23
31.	Major change in working hours or conditions	20
32.	Change in residence	20
33.	Changing to a new school	20
34.	Major change in usual type and/or amount of recreation	19
35.	Major change in church activities (e.g., a lot more or less than usual)	19
36.	Major change in social activities (e.g., clubs, dancing, movies, visiting, etc.)	18
37.	Taking on a mortgage or loan less than $10,000 (e.g., purchasing a car, TV, freezer, etc.)	17
38.	Major change in sleeping habits (a lot more or a lot less sleep, or change in part of day when asleep)	16
39.	Major change in number of family get-togethers (e.g., a lot more or a lot less than usual)	15
40.	Major change in eating habits (a lot more or a lot less food intake, or very different meal hours or surroundings)	15
41.	Vacation	13
42.	Christmas	12
43.	Minor violations of the law (e.g., traffic tickets, jaywalking, disturbing the peace, etc.)	11

Source: Thomas Holmes and Richard Rahe, "Holmes-Rahe Social Readjustment Rating Scale," *Journal of Psychosomatic Research,* vol. II, 1967.

Dealing with the Problems of Contemporary Marriage

chapter 7

As Hall and Hall (1980) suggest: "The traditional family model of the husband as breadwinner and wife as homemaker, together 'till death do us part,' is becoming a vestige of a past society." According to the U.S. Labor Department, the traditional "typical American family" with a working husband, a homemaker wife, and two children, now makes up only 7 percent of the nation's families. In addition, in 1975, 44 percent of all married women were working, as were 37 percent of women with children under six; in 1960, the comparable figures were 31 percent and 19 percent, respectively. It is this development more than any other which many sociologists and psychologists are claiming is responsible for the doubling of the divorce rate over the last ten years in the U.S. and many other countries in the West. Indeed, in a review of research literature on marital adjustment in dual-career marriages, Staines, Pleck, Shepard, and O'Connor (1979) found that of the thirteen major studies in this area, using either a national U.S. sample or a community-wide sample, at least eleven of them showed that marital adjustment was worse for dual-career wives than for nonworking wives. This is not to say that this development is an unworthy one, but rather to acknowledge the reality that social change of this sort, *in the short-term,* is likely to lead to a great deal of stress within the family, and ultimately in the individual's worklife. The problem stems primarily from our earlier discussion of the family as a social support system, which we suggested provides the breadwinning husband with a "safe haven" after the pressures of everyday worklife—or at least that is what he has come to expect. Jean Renshaw (1977) puts this current dilemma succinctly: "According to traditional corporate mythology, the ideal family is a support system to help each employee carry out company policy. Each morning the executive emerges from his domestic cocoon, refreshed and ready to do battle in the business world. In the evening, he returns to the family haven for solace, support, and refurbishment. If this was ever the reality, it is no longer; and the illusion is becoming increasingly difficult to maintain." She goes on to liken this traditional conception of the family to a missile system with the company as the *command module* and the family as the *support system.* In this system, she suggests "Message direction is fixed: control messages travel down; support and nourishment messages travel up. Inputs come from the environment of the corporation, not from feedback or give and take. The command module has the important information and 'knows best'." But, as we all know, the worlds of work and home are interdependent and one set of decisions reached at work may very easily affect the home environment, and, likewise, changes in the marital situation are also likely to affect the work environment. It is because of this complex set of interactions and the contemporary movement toward dual-career marriages and its contribution to weakening of the family unit that makes an understanding of various marital roles essential. In this chapter we discuss a number of different typologies of family structure and their effects on various family members. In addition, we hope to provide the reader with some suggestions about ways of dealing with the inevitable consequences of the "changing family."

Different Types of Family Structure

Handy (1978) has come up with an interesting typology of marriage patterns, based on his research looking at husbands and wives in terms of their needs for achievement, dominance, affiliation, and nurturance. As can be seen in Figure 7.1, he combined "achievement" and "dominance" needs and "affiliation" and "nurturance" needs and came up with four quadrants in terms of primary approaches to life. To arrive at particular *marriage patterns,* he combined the husbands' orientations with the wives'.

Although there are sixteen logically possible combinations of marriage patterns, he found only eight turned up in his in-

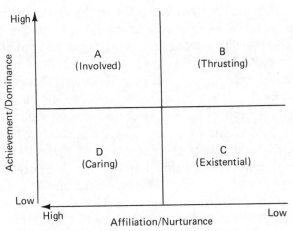

FIGURE 7.1 Types of Marriages

Source: C. Handy, "The Family: Help or Hindrance," in C.L. Cooper and R. Payne, *Stress at Work* (New York and London: John Wiley & Sons, 1978).

vestigations and only four principal patterns. Let's look at his four most frequent ones. Pattern one was of a *"thrusting* husband and a *caring* wife," which Handy found to be the most frequent one and the one which represents the traditional sex role stereotype. Here the husband is the breadwinner and the wife the homemaker. His goals of success and achievement are her goals as well, and all her efforts are involved in the home and providing him with support, although she is not particularly interested in the details of his work. These marriages were predictable, structured, and created little stress. Although Handy found this marriage to still be in the majority, the prospects for its future survival are bleak.

The negative aspects of this pattern are that the wife has difficulty in expressing or meeting her own needs while her children are young and also finds it difficult to cope when the children leave home or the husband's career reaches its ceiling, or indeed, deteriorates.

The second marriage pattern is "the pairing of two thrusters." In this pattern, both the husband and the wife have high needs for achievement and dominance. In the past, the high thrusting wife tended to stay at home and either be frustrated at not achieving her own goals or attempt to meet her achievement need in homemaking activities. Thrusters usually desire support or the "caring" role, and if both are making this demand known, it can generate considerable discontent. This is also the pairing situation most likely to lead to dual-career families with the changing conception of woman's role in the home. Naturally, if both thrusters become thoroughly involved in their worklife, as they are likely to do, their domestic arrangements and circumstance are likely to be very chaotic indeed. Since, by definition, thrusters need the comforts of the home environment—whether husband or wife thruster—the conflicts, tensions, and stress in the family will be enormous. In addition, these types of relationships become very much more strained when children arrive on the scene because the thrusting husband attempts to get his wife to play out the traditional sex role stereotype (i.e., she must give up her job) and draws on the guilt he knows his wife has buried just below the surface of her emancipation.

The third pattern is the partnership of two "involved" people. Although the husband and wife are both high achievers with a tendency to be dominant in their interpersonal relationships, they also place a high value on "caring" and "belonging." As Handy suggests: "They prefer to share arenas, not separate them." The stress level in these marriages is very high, since both partners have an underlying "thrusting" instinct, but this is tempered with a "caring" element that encourages them to confront one another with problems. In contrast, two "thrusters" would avoid resolution by compromise and discussion, and would seek victory through defeat. Although one partner or the other may have to do something in the short run that he/she would prefer not to, there is sufficient flexibility in the marriage to provide short-term support, so that he/she can end up doing what either wants to do in the longer term.

And finally, the last marriage pattern is "involved husband" with a "caring wife." Here the husband is highly achievement-oriented but also values the caring aspect of relationships. The husband is likely to be under a great deal of stress, since not only is he ambitious, but he also cares about other people and is very concerned not to hurt others. Because the husband is sensitive to others' feelings, he feels guilty when his wife commits herself solely to him (although he does want her social support). As Handy suggests these relationships are "less predictable and the tensions less well contained. These relationships are more intense and emotional. There is more questioning and more effort to rework roles than in the traditional marriages."

The following general points can be offered in respect to Handy's framework and its effect on family stress:

1. "That where the activity pattern of a marriage fits that which would normally be required by the underlying *mix of personalities* there

will be less 'familial' stress." For example, if an A-A couple were forced by the success of the husband and the needs of the children to adopt a B-D pattern, family stress is likely to be increased.

2. If the pattern of husband-wife relationship didn't change with changes in the *central life interests* of each member, there is liable to be more family stress.

3. If there are changes in the activity pattern at home or work which do not fit with one of the satisfactory marriage patterns above, "then either the job or the attitudes or the partners must change if stress and conflict is to be avoided."

A not too dissimilar categorization of marriages was recently advanced by Francine and Tim Hall (1979) in their excellent book *The Two Career Couple*. Incidentally, they define the two career couple as "two people who share a lifestyle that includes (1) cohabitation, (2) separate work roles for both partners, and (3) a love relationship that supports and facilitates both." They contend that there are four dual-career family role structures: accommodators, adversaries, allies, and acrobats. The *accommodator* pattern usually has one partner who is high in career involvement and low in home involvement, while the other partner is high in home involvement and low in career involvement. The difference between this pattern and the traditional family one (or Handy's first type) is that either sex can play either role. The possible stresses and strains are kept to a minimum. There are an increasing number of men prepared to play the traditional female role, while his wife becomes the breadwinner—although the movement in this direction is insignificant in comparison to the number of families with working husbands and wives.

The *adversaries,* on the other hand, are very much the two working thrusters, a couple in which "both partners are highly involved in their careers, and have low involvement in home, family, or partner support roles." As in the two thruster marriages, this is the most stressful marital pattern, where there is competition over priorities, avoidance of nonwork roles in the family, conflict in terms of career development of either member, and the unwillingness to give up any of their career identity to meet the needs of husband/wife or the family unit (unless the "work costs" are negligible).

The third type is the *allies* pattern in which "two people are both highly involved in either career or home and family roles, with little identity tied up in the other." This is broken down into two different orientations, which they refer to as Type IIIa and IIIb couples. In the former, both partners don't identify with their careers and derive their primary satisfaction from their family and their relationship. Type IIIb, on the other hand, identify strongly with their jobs and not the family, "their identities are not tied up in having a well ordered home, gourmet dinners, entertaining, or often, children. The support structure may be 'purchased', in dinners out, maids, and catering services, or simply do not exist." The potential stress problem in the latter case is that the couple doesn't have the time to spend on the relationship that it requires to maintain it as a support base for their independent activities.

The fourth type of couple is the *acrobats.* As the name implies this type of couple is made up of partners who are highly involved in all their roles, both work and family. They perceive the home and work roles as equally important and therefore are very vulnerable to overload. As the Halls suggest, their major source of stress derives from the "conflict of trying to meet all the demands—having a successful career, being a good partner, having a well ordered home, providing real and emotional support for the spouse, and still finding time for the relationship." As more and more women attempt to meet their own needs in the workplace, the more difficult an *acrobatic marriage* will be.

How to Cope with Dual-Career Families and Their Problems

As we begin to move increasingly away from an accommodator-type marriage pattern to any of the others described by the Halls, we will find that the potential pressures in life will also increase at an exponential rate, depending on the type of pattern adopted. A number of people involved in this field have suggested a number of strategies. Bailyn (1970) suggested that there are three strategies available to reduce the complexity of a marriage pattern based on the principle of equal sharing. First, she posits the most obvious solution—*"limitation* of both partners' involvement in one or the other area." By this she means that some form of role negotiation should take place whereby specific limitations for each member should be negotiated. If, for example, neither member is prepared to accommodate the other's needs in terms of home commitments, it might be usefully agreed to lessen family demands by having a smaller family or no family at all. In a work context it might mean negotiating more flexible work hours, or reducing time commitments, or sharing jobs. What is being done here, in effect, is limiting the demands from either or both areas of life in a way that allows both partners an opportunity to cope in two worlds. Second, she suggests the notion of *recycling,* which is "a shift in the staging of work and family events." The main purpose of this is to organize events in such a way that work and home demands do not occur simultaneously or at least that the maximal demands do not overlap. This may mean that one member of the family has to delay a particular activity, be it an educational or occupational one, to a later period of the family's life cycle. It involves a great deal of long-term planning and the willingness to give up current interests and motivations to perhaps later stages in one's life. Bailyn continually indicates that the success of any of these strategies is highly contingent on the partners' ability and willingness to accommodate to the other and the family unit as a whole. And finally, she suggests *segmentation* as an approach to reduce complexity in dual-career marriages. This is defined as the process of "strengthening the boundaries between family and work: by compartmentalizing each area so that one does not have to deal with family and work issues at the same time." By making sure that one's world of work is dealt with during the 9 to 5 working day, it frees up the individual to deal exclusively with family issues and problems at other times. This might extend to seeking out the type of employment and careers that will allow this. Once again the effort here is to plan activities so that they occur sequentially instead of simultaneously, thereby reducing the problems of overload or role conflict.

Bailyn's suggestions fit in nicely with what the Halls highlight as the three main stressors among two-career couples: overload, conflict, and change. They use examples we could all identify with, for example, one of their couples described their *overload* as follows: "When we're both under the gun at work, there's just no energy left for anything else. The apartment can go for a while, but what hurts is that neither of us has anything left at the end of the day for the other. At times like that there just isn't any support for anything or anyone. I don't know how people with kids handle it." Or when there is a *conflict* of work and lifestyles: "He is pulling back, putting more energy into relaxing. He wants me to play racquetball with him, but I come home late, have evening meetings, travel. I'm just getting my career launched, and he is cutting back on his. This has created a real problem for us—we're just coming from different directions. It's causing real strain in our relationship." This will be a particular problem for those who adopt Bailyn's *recycling* strategy, which may inevitably lead to more synchronized workloads but also to differences in interest and direction at any given moment in time.

The Halls feel that the main answer to the problems experienced by two-career couples is to develop a new career orientation and style, an approach they term *the protean career* (the term protean comes from the Greek mythological figure Proteus, who was able to change his form at will). They define (Hall and Hall, 1980) the protean career as "a process which the person, not the organization, is managing. It consists of all the person's varied experiences in education, training, work in several organizations, changes in occupational field, etc. The protean career is *not* what happens to the person in any one organization. The protean person's own personal career choices and search for self-fulfillment are the unifying or integrative elements in his or her life. The criterion of success is internal (psychological success), not external. In short, the protean career is shaped more by the individual than by the organization and may be redirected from time to time to meet the needs of the person." What the Halls are really saying is that one must take care of his/her career, that is, they ought to develop (in light of their particular combination of needs) career plans for themselves rather than accept the inevitable organizational career paths and timetables. Once again the emphasis is on planning and self-determination.

What the Organization Can Do to Help Dual-Career Families

So far we have looked at what individuals can do to help themselves; how they can plan their own future. Much of this has been suggested on the assumption that organizational life will stay fundamentally the same, that is, that work organizations are not likely to acknowledge the development of two-career families in practical terms in the workplace. This may or may not be the case, but it is still important to assist organizations to understand the kinds of strategies that might help them to minimize the problems of their dual-career employees and prepare a firmer foundation to alleviate home-work interface stresses and strains.

Flexible Working Arrangements. There are a wide range of flexible working arrangements that organizations can provide their male and female employees that can help them to accommodate to changing family patterns. *Flexitime* is obviously one good example. In order that a dual wife or husband can meet the psychological responsibilities associated with their children's education, or indeed, free themselves of guilt, many parents feel that they must take their children to school and/or pick them up. This is very difficult to accomplish under the current 9 to 5 (or later) arrangement, and would be made much easier under flexitime conditions—as long as it was applicable for both husband and wife. Flexitime is not only useful during the work week, but why shouldn't it be extended to "school vacation" times? Many dual-career parents are concerned about arrangements for their children during the summer months when they are at home. There are several ways of coping with this problem: allowing the dual wife or husband to have a lighter load during these months, allowing them to build up a backlog of working time during other months to relieve them during these; providing facilities on site during the summer months for young children (perhaps by the use of university students training in the field of primary education), or some combination of these.

Another more flexible working arrangement would be more *part-time work* in a variety of different forms: limiting the number of days a week, or hours in a day, or indeed in shortening the work week by allowing individuals to work three or four day, forty-hour weeks. This last suggestion is growing in popularity and if dual husband and wife were able to do this they could, by careful planning, easily manage their domestic and work arrangements between them. In 1972 an American Management Association survey estimated that between 700 and 1,000 firms of over 100,000 employees *in toto* were on a four day, forty-hour week in the U.S. By 1975, the number of firms grew to 3,000 covering over one million workers. Indeed, many firms are moving to a three day, thirty-eight-hour week without decline in productivity and job satisfaction (Foster et al., 1979).

Allied to many of these suggestions is the notion that organizations provide *creche or nursery facilities* in the workplace. There is increasing growth of these in many of the "advanced thinking" organizations. Many educationalists and psychologists have felt this is a good idea, since it provides the mother or father with the opportunity of seeing their children some time during working hours. A less satisfactory solution would be community-based nurseries, but these may be necessary for those who work for small companies or who are self-employed. The benefits that organizations could derive from the introduction of the industrial *kibbutzim* in the U.S. and in Europe seems so obvious that it is surprising that more companies have not followed suit.

Working at Home. With the advent of the microprocessor revolution, it should become increasingly easier for dual husbands and wives in certain types of jobs to work at home. The need for a central workplace should decrease quite dramatically over the next decade or two. Already, employees can take home a computer terminal or indeed a minicomputer itself to carry out many of the tasks that they were once only able to do in a centralized work environment. In order to be able to do this, work organizations will have to rid themselves of their deep-rooted, nefarious suspicion of their fellow workers, that is, that they will take every opportunity to exploit their employer and work as little as possible; and only by *overseeing* them will work get done! Indeed it is this very *control* that has made the process of work for many unsatisfying and has encouraged the compartmentalization of work and homelife to the detriment of the former. As C. Wright Mills has suggested: "Each day men sell little pieces of themselves in order to try and buy them back each night and weekend with little pieces of fun."

Some organizations may one day realize that they may not need a centralized workplace at all. For the time being, however, work organizations ought to explore the variety of jobs that could easily be done at home and provide this degree of flexibility to their employees. At the very least, it is worth an experiment!

Smoothing the Way for Women. Many women who have played the traditional family "caring" role, need particular help if they are to change the pattern of their marriage and fulfill a more dual role. One problem these women may face, after many years away from work, is *lack of confidence* and feeling that they are out-of-date (or, in fact, actually *are* out-of-date). It is in the interest of employers and the wider community to provide opportunities for these sorts of women to be brought up-to-date with current developments. This might best be done by professional associations or indeed by work organizations providing updating courses for ex-employees who have temporarily left employment to raise a family. As Michael Fogarty (1971) has suggested: "The important thing in the interests of both employers and of young mothers themselves is to minimize the interruption to a highly qualified woman's career and to keep her as closely in touch as possible with her particular world of work." Any help the industrial organization can give its former employees in maintaining their skills may pay off greatly in the future, not only in terms of "goodwill" but also in reducing costs of retraining or initial training of needed new staff. As far as the question of confidence is concerned, this can be done during the updating activity or by specialized courses prior to retraining or updating, depending on the time gap between the termination of full employment and the return.

Maternity and Paternity Leave. It is obvious that what many women at work need, if they are preparing to have a family, is some sense of security about their job. In this respect it only seems sensible to have some reasonable maternity leave with a guaranteed right to return to work after it, and with some financial security during the leave period. Most countries in the European Common Market have guarantees against dismissal during pregnancy, a guarantee of paid maternity leave (usually between eight to twelve weeks and up to six months in many Eastern European countries) and guarantees of the right to return to work either immediately following the paid maternity leave period or unpaid leave after some prearranged return period (in some cases up to two or three years later). Different countries have different arrangements in this respect.

Paternity leave is also particularly important in the changing circumstance of the family. Few organizations provide this contemporary innovation, but many will have to consider it in the near future if they want to more systematically deal with what may end up, if ignored, an uncontrolled absenteeism problem in the future. Dual-career families will increasingly need the flexibility of short-leave periods, and the provision of leave for both men and women should help to ease the problem.

Mobile Lifestyle and the Family

Not only are we vulnerable to the stresses and strains of life as a result of the changing pattern of marriages, but also to the increasingly "mobile lifestyle" we have adopted, which is partly due, once again, to the organizations we work for. This phenomenon is particularly true of white-collar workers, who in the United States and Europe are shifting jobs and homes at a much greater rate than just two decades ago. Indeed, mobility is now an almost inescapable fact of working life. Pahl and Pahl (1971) reported that 22 percent of their sample of British managers had moved workplace (and home) every two or three years and a further 33 percent once every four or five years. In the United States, 66 percent of the managers studied by Seidenberg (1973) expected to move about every two or three years. It has been suggested by many psychologists and sociologists that this mobility is contributing considerably to various forms of stress-related illness, alcoholism, and mental disorders.

There are a number of reasons why mobility may be stressful. Glaser and Strauss (1969) suggest, for example, that it depends on a number of important variables: whether or not the move is reversible; what time factors are involved; whether one or many status changes occur at one time; whether it is a group or individual event; and whether there are generally accepted rules to guide the "travelers."

Nevertheless, increasing mobility in Western society is creating difficulties for the individual and family unit. In this respect the author and a colleague, Dr. Judi Marshall, did a major study among white-collar and managerial staff to see what the effect of job and home mobility had on the individual and his family (Cooper and Marshall, 1978). Our sample comprised of very senior managers in a multinational company and were almost entirely male (which reflects the difficulty women currently face in achieving top management jobs in most large industrial companies.) We explored the factors that created and attenuated stress for the managers and their wives before, during, and after a job (and home) relocation. From this one can see the difficulties the increasingly mobile family is having to face at each stage of their nomadic existence.

Before the Move. In the period of time preceding a move, there are doubts in the minds of both husband and wife about the uncertain nature of the new job and community they will be moving to. Since wives tend to become more involved in the local community than their husbands, and it is from such contacts that she derives her separate identity, she may be loath to give this up and have to start again in a new location (Seidenberg, 1973). Family ties in the area they are moving from can also create problems during this period. "Deserting" elderly parents can be a source of guilt, particularly if there are no other relatives nearby to take care of them.

As far as children are concerned, three factors appear to be particularly important in the context of moving: the *immediate emotional environment* created by their parents (as they try to cope with uncertainty), *education,* and *friendships.* In general, children prefer stability to change and uncertainty. When parents are worrying in advance about how they will cope with

TABLE 7.1 Factors Which Accentuate or Attenuate the Stress Involved in Moving

	White-collar Professional	
Before the Move	During the Move	After the Move
MINUS	MINUS	MINUS
Happy in previous job	Extra physical demands of travel and extra work	New job makes excessive demands
Reservations about new job (e.g., lateral transfer, no salary increase)	House hunting is difficult and uncertain	Interpersonal problems at work
Doubts ability to master new job	Has to travel on business at time of move	Lacks skills new job requires
Wife reluctant to move (e.g., leaving friends or her job)	Separation	Needs to prove himself quickly
Children at important stage of education	Wife and children unhappy at his absence	Worried that unable to afford new mortgage
Family regard present area as home	Wife jealous of his freedom from responsibility	Concerned because wife and children having problems adapting
Worried about effects on wife and children	Finds it difficult to balance competing demands on his time and interest	Area doesn't offer desired facilities (e.g., sports)
PLUS	PLUS	PLUS
Happy about new job (it was for promotion, etc.)	Enjoys freedom and "bachelor" social life	Job goes well and is satisfying
Loss of motivation for previous job	Involved in new job	New work team provide support
Wife eager to move	House transactions accomplished relatively easily and quickly	Family adapt relatively easily
The move brings benefits to the family (a new house, better schooling)	Makes money on the exchange	

The Wife

Before the Move	During the Move	After the Move
MINUS	**MINUS**	**MINUS**
Dislikes upheaval and change	Has to cope with a lot of extra work	Feels lonely and isolated (misses old friends and doesn't make new ones)
Involved in local community	Misses husband	Locals are hostile to strangers
Likes current house	Finds she has little social support in the area	New house unsatisfactory or needs tiring alterations
Works outside the home	Feels that husband does not appreciate her problems, is jealous of his freedom	Dislikes characteristics of the area
Children at critical stage of education	Children upset and miss their father	Husband too involved in new job to give support
Children reluctant to move or react badly to change (she worries about their ability to cope)	House hunting and timing of move are uncertain and exhausting	No job opportunities for her
Lives near her parents		Lives further away from parents
		Children have problems at school (slow to make new friends)
		Husband unhappy in new job
PLUS	**PLUS**	**PLUS**
Dislikes current situation (geographic area, house, etc.)	Friends rally round	Befriended by neighbor or company wife
Enjoys change and seeing new places	Separation kept to a minimum by easy transactions, etc.	Already has friends in the area
Likes proposed new location (has friends there)	Finds she can cope and takes pride in her new independence	Makes friends via established channels (the church baby-sitting club, etc.)
Children will benefit (better quality schooling, can start again if problems at school or with social lives)		Husband and children adapt easily and quickly
		Moves nearer to parents

the upheaval of the moving period itself, and later with establishing a life in the new community, children sense the insecurity and are adversely affected. It is important for mobile families to keep this in mind when next involved in a relocation —either by sharing their own anxieties *directly* with their children or by creating some *security* buffer for those too young to understand.

There are a host of other problems which crop up during this stage of any move, for example, many homemaking/ "caring" wives will be reluctant to leave the house they have helped to build and create. Indeed, sociologists have gone so far as to compare the grief at loss of house to bereavement (Fried, 1965). It is the little things that become important—leaving behind the flowers which have just been planted or the specially made or designed fittings, and so on.

In addition, this period places a great deal of pressure on wives since they are usually the ones who have to handle the mechanics of the move, while the husband is working or has indeed taken up residence in the new job. She is expected not only to handle the house sale, removal arrangements, etc., but also to be the reservoir of social support for her husband and children.

The Move. Compared to phase one, during which the load was mainly emotional uncertainty, this is a period of intense activity. In addition, it is a time when the husband has left to take up the new job, while the wife remains to settle the domestic arrangements. The husband's main preoccupations are trying to get established in his job, trying to cope with home vs. work demands at a distance, etc. We found in our study that the women suffer three major practical worries during this stage: arranging the sale of the current house, participating at a distance in buying "a replacement," and organizing new schools for the children. The wife's practical difficulties are often aggravated by two further problems: (1) uncertainty regarding the timing of the move, and (2) her own attitudes, reservations about moving, and nagging suspicion that her husband is enjoying a new freedom which she cannot share. For many couples who are separated during this period (he in the new and she in the old location), the complex of pressures makes their weekends together highly disturbing and unsatisfactory.

For most couples the first few months of separation are the worst. After this, events usually develop to make the situation more acceptable.

1. A routine becomes established.

2. Children settle down and discover that their father does come back after each desertion.

3. The novelty of the husband's freedom wears off slightly and he comes to miss, and express more concern about regaining, his home comforts.

4. House transactions become more definite and encouraging.

5. The wife discovers that she can cope and takes a pride in her new found independence and decision-making capacity.

Separation represents a real crisis point in most marriages, however many times it has been experienced in the past. It is a period of redefining roles and confirming (or denying) emotional commitments. In many relationships this stressful interlude can have substantial growthful effects; in others, however, it can serve to generate a distance and conflict which the couple take some time to resolve.

After the Move. During this phase the family is settling into the new location, the breadwinning white-collar worker is adjusting to his new job and home, while the wife is trying to create a new home and school environment for the children. This is a difficult period for the wife and children because they have to devote some of their effort at creating friends and community contacts, particularly the wife. The homemaking wife usually finds it a lonely period. Many wives in our study indicated that they were depressed and isolated for the first few months, wandering from shop to shop to keep themselves busy and creating any opportunity of meeting neighbors. This frequently reflects itself in her relationship with her husband, and a vicious stress feedback loop forms. Indeed, most of the couples we interviewed agreed that "moving takes a year out of your life," but after that period most people settle into a routine and things are once again back to some semblance of stability.

Moving and the Life Cycle

We have been looking at mobility in terms of the "average" white-collar family, but people experience different problems in respect to job (and home) relocation depending where they are in their life cycle, as Marshall and Cooper (1976) found.

The Single Person. Moving has its problems for the single man or woman, but they are few compared to those at later life stages. His or her main concern is the job and being seen to do well in it (at a critical and well-watched phase). Other potential pressures are the "culture-shock" of starting work after life at university, having no separate world to retire to in the evenings to help one switch off, the problems of house-hunting, being lonely in a strange town (often peopled mainly by 'contented' married couples), and trying to maintain contact with old friends (including a possible future husband/wife). On the other hand, moving around has considerable benefits. It provides an opportunity to see new places as well as to gain experience which will stand him/her in good stead in the future.

The Young Married. With marriage, moving usually becomes easier, because the individual now has someone with whom to share the tasks, disappointments, and successes involved. "We were not long married and everything was exciting" captures the general attitude. Even living in a disliked area of the country is tolerated if there are compensations and the stay is not seen as being "for life." Again, the breadwinner's job dominates. In dual-career marriages in which the wife continues to work, she is less likely to suffer the loneliness which was the main problem for the preceding generation. This is usually an active and satisfying time for the couple socially, as well as a busy one for those who enjoy home-improving and decorating.

Married, with a Young Family. House-hunting now becomes a major problem both because the wife is too tied down to participate much and because house choice becomes more crucial and criteria more exacting. Size, nearness to schools and shops and, as the wife is now housebound (in the traditional family), potential friends must all be considered. Separation, which because of the practical problems involved usually lasts longer than at earlier life stages, is an emotionally draining time for all the family. The wife's adaptation to and happiness in her new environment become critical factors. The couple find it harder to make out-of-work friends, tied down as they are, and more emphasis is placed on nearness (the neighbors) and "same boat" acquaintances (e.g., couples with children of the same age and interests). Housing can be a vital factor here and many choose to live on modern housing estates where they can be with "their own kind."

Preschool children are relatively no problem to move compared to those over five-years-old for whom education becomes important. Having to arrange schooling now becomes a major factor, particularly for five- and eleven-year-olds, and for many this is the main determining factor of house location and the timing of the move.

The white-collar worker's job, while sometimes unsatisfactory, is usually as much a stabilizing as a disruptive factor in moving. It gives him something to do during the day, provides a ready-made system of contacts and potential friends, and opens substantial opportunities for achievement and satisfaction. Compared to this, his wife is at a considerable disadvantage and has to start from scratch to build up a new life. Most managers agree that it is she who "bears the brunt of moving."

At this stage, relocation is welcomed more for its long- than its short-term advantages—the manager's promotion, moving to a better house, improving a previously unsatisfactory situation and "getting out of a rut" are some of its more frequently quoted benefits. If moves come too frequently, as they sometimes do at this formative career stage, this can in itself be a source of stress (especially to the wife), irrespective of the particular details. Couples begin to develop strategies to cope with repeated disruptions. Packard (1972) suggests that American managers and their wives become adept at "instant gregariousness"; Pahl and Pahl (1971) feel that the British reaction is characteristically more "reserved" and that many mobiles retreat into their nuclear family.

Married, with a Teenaged Family. Moving now affects the fates of (say) four, rather than two, adult individuals, all of whom will probably become actively involved in the initial decision. The white-collar professional and his wife are now only repeating familiar, if at times still painful, procedures, and their main concern will be the satisfaction of their childrens' needs. Continuity of schooling and making friends are the most critical factors. Relocation difficulties can make adolescence an even more turbulent time than would normally be expected. Often teenagers react with resentment and rebellion at the thought of moving, especially if they have lived long enough in one place to think of it as "home," with all the word implies. Usually, however, they settle down relatively easily in the new community and appear to benefit from a lesson in adaptability.

The Empty Nest. Most of those who are still moving at this life stage have come to regard mobility as an acceptable and natural way of life. It is likely to be a sign that the husband is successful in his job and this will be a source of satisfaction to both partners. They may find that repeated moving has prevented them from becoming (and discouraged them from wanting to become) involved in the local communities through which they have passed. It will, however, also have given them friends all over the country so that they seldom have to start from scratch in establishing the level of contact they do desire. Many do express some concern that they never settle down anywhere and that they are not providing a stable focus for their now also mobile children and grandchildren to refer to and visit. Where to retire becomes a problem for those who have lived in so many places but belonged to none.

Table 7.2 summarizes the conclusions of this section

TABLE 7.2 Predominant Relocation Stressors at Different Life Stages

	Single	*Married*			
		No Children	*Young Children*	*Older Children*	*Empty Nest*
The job	√				
Separation from family			√		
Housing			√	√	
Wife's reluctance to move			√	√	
Wife's adaptation to new environment		√	√		
Children				√	√
Education			√	√	
Responsibilities to parents					√
Social life	√		√		

showing the predominant problems at each of the various life stages.

Moving with a Career-Oriented Wife. Mobility in phase with the husband's career progress makes it almost impossible for the wife to develop a working life of her own. She will have difficulty seeing any necessary training courses through to the end, may have to leave a job she enjoys and start again at the bottom of the ladder elsewhere, and often finds that there are no jobs in her field in the new location. Having to mark time for six months or so while she sees to the chores of moving is both an added aggravation and makes her even less desirable as a prospective employee when she is free to look for work. (A further negative qualification at this stage is that she cannot guarantee she will not soon be moved again.) A previous "safe bet" in such trying circumstances was teaching. It was eminently transferable and also by nature part-time, fitting in well with commitments to the rest of the family. This is no longer such an easy option; not only have qualification requirements become more rigorous, there are now few vacancies in the profession.

So what can the dual wife do? At the moment she has three basic options. The first is to decide that her husband's job comes first and fit any work opportunities she has around its requirements, probably hoping to return to full-time employment at a later, more stable life stage. She may in the meantime divert her energies to being a housewife/mother and casual voluntary worker. At the other extreme is the wife who succeeds in developing her own career. There are currently few who come into this category, although as we discussed they are on the increase. Rapoport and Rapoport (1976) describe some of the elaborate support systems dual-career families need to be able to maintain their chosen lifestyle; an almost essential ingredient is that the husband should stay in one place. Today's young white-collar professionals are reported to be much less willing than previous generations to move within companies—

having to satisfy their wife's as well as their own career needs is likely to be one of the main reasons behind this trend. Between those two pure options comes the third—the broad band of compromise. Many couples are trying to achieve the best of both worlds, letting the man's promotion opportunities (perhaps in the future it will even be the woman's) dictate their pattern of movement, but looking for a satisfying job for the wife in each new location. This is by no means easy, especially since the wife must usually start from scratch in each position (her husband's within-company transfer is more of a progression), usually after a break from work in which she has been busy moving. Today's young mobile wife is in the same relationship to her job that her predecessor was to her home and social life; for both relocation means a disruptive end and a traumatic beginning. If she adds "mother" to her repertoire of roles, the dual wife stands even less chance of achieving any work ambitions she may have. Her husband is in a difficult, ambivalent position in this respect. While he may well sympathize with her problems, he is likely to be extremely conscious of the benefits to him firstly of relocation (for the promotion, new job challenge, etc., it brings); and secondly, of her being forced into the supportive housewife role.

It is interesting to speculate where current trends will lead us. Their immediate consequences seem to be an increasing number of childless marriages. Farid (1974) reports a postponement in young couples' starting their families or adding to them, a decline in mean ultimate family size for women married since 1964, and a growing number of young executives who are less than wholly dedicated to the companies they work for (and to working *per se*?), and who place a compensatingly greater emphasis on having a satisfying family life and helping their wives satisfy their own career needs. As men and women experiment with their own and each others' roles, the balance of power is shifting not only within the family but also within the companies which employ its members. Male white-collar workers seem to be setting themselves lower ambitions, while their wives strive to fill three highly demanding roles simultaneously. Companies with an eye to the future must keep abreast of these developments if they are to retain the loyalty of their employees and know what rewards to offer in the future and *to whom.*

STRATEGIES FOR RELIEVING STRESS AT WORK
part III

What the Organization Can Do to Cope with Stress
chapter 8

Causes and Sources of Stress

Cooper and Marshall (1978; 1979) have identified a long list of causal factors in work stress, which can be conveniently grouped under the seven headings discussed in Chapter 2 (see Figure 8.1). This should not be taken as a simple list of factors to be eliminated, because the grouping includes factors that are essential for any sort of achievement, and the removal of one—for example, too much work—can result in simply producing the opposite which is equally stressful—that is, too little work. Furthermore, there is the inescapable paradox that stress to one man is satisfaction to another. For some, the lack of job security is a stimulus to the satisfaction of living dangerously; for others, the existence of tight deadlines is the challenge in their job that provides the greatest satisfaction. Lazarus (1967) has demonstrated that a stressful situation cannot be defined by reference to objective criteria. Only the individual can define his own stressors as a result of his own experience and apprehensions,

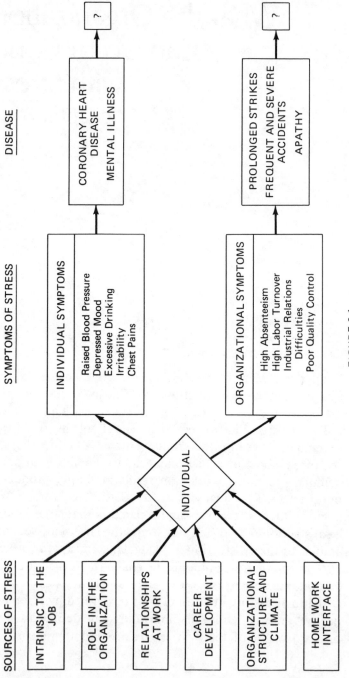

FIGURE 8.1

and for each individual there will be a range of potential factors that will put him under stress. "Stimulating pressure" will change to "debilitating stress" when the individual feels unable to cope, becomes anxious about that "feeling of inability" and begins to adopt defensive behaviors.

Coping with Stress

Once the individual experiences his stress, he will adopt a series of behaviors in reaction to it. In most cases these will be adaptive behaviors dealing directly with the stressful situation by producing solutions to it. Typical stressors and adaptive behaviors might be:

Stressor	*Adaptive Behavior*
Overworked	Some work delegated
Not aware of company policy on a particular matter	Finds out what policy is
Poor working relationship with colleague	Confronts issue with colleague and negotiates better relationship
Underpromotion	Leaves organization for another
Company vs. family demands	Takes a holiday
Role ambiguity	Seeks clarification with colleagues or superior

Each of these tackles the basic cause of the stress and solves it, at least temporarily and perhaps permanently.

An alternative set of behaviors are those which are maladaptive in that they do not deal with the problem; they avoid it and probably aggravate it. Typical of these might be:

Stressor	*Maladaptive Behavior*
Overworked	Accepts work overload with result that general performance deteriorates
Not aware of company policy on a particular matter	Guesses incorrectly and performs inappropriately

Poor working relationship with colleague	Attacks colleague indirectly through third party
Underpromotion	Loses confidence and becomes convinced of own inadequacy
Company vs. family demands	Blames company for family discontent
Role ambiguity	Withdraws from some aspects of work role

In all these situations the initiator is always the individual under stress and it is reasonable to suggest that an external intervention is only going to become potentially useful as a way of altering maladaptive behaviors, which harm both the individual and his organization, into adaptive behaviors.

The Problem of the External Initiative

External initiatives to assist a stressed individual may come from a number of sources and an agent of the employing organization, such as a personnel officer, may be the least likely to succeed. This is in part because the individual may not realize that the organization is the source of his problem or because it actually derives from a combination of sources (e.g., an overbearing boss *and* a disgruntled wife). Partly it is because of the widespread reluctance of individuals to acknowledge that they are under stress at all. The reasons for this can be attributed to a variety of cultural factors such as conventional assumptions about "proper behavior." Many of the middle-class British, for example, like to ascribe to themselves such attributes as stiff upper lip, sang-froid, imperturbable, unflappable, and self-reliant. All have the self-illusion or self-assurance of being able to cope with stressful situations and a feeling of disapproval or condescension about those who are not able to cope and are, by extension, "dependent, weak, and lacking in moral fibre." Acknowledging a difficulty in coping with stress is likely to be seen as a severe loss of face. The situation in the United States appears to be at least superficially different, with a larger proportion of the population utilizing the "helping professions" (e.g., psychotherapy, counseling, experiential learning groups, etc.). Nevertheless, there is still a reluctance in business to accept stress as an inevitable consequence of organizational life. This degree of inhibition in "owning up" to being under stress is the main problem of the external intervention and means that a range of interventions from outside the organization may be more likely to succeed. An individual may seek or accept intervention from a spouse, family doctor, priest, parent, marriage guidance counselor, friend, or lawyer more readily than from his employing organization.

The Scope for Personnel Intervention

Within the framework thusfar presented, and with the reservations that have been mentioned, we now move to consider a range of interventions that could come from the personnel specialists within an organization. They are grouped under two headings:

1. OPERATIONAL: These strategies modify existing personnel operations to take account of their potential for stress mitigation.
2. INFLUENTIAL: These refer to the potential for stress mitigation second-hand, through the influence of personnel specialists on overall management philosophy and policy.

OPERATIONAL: IMMEDIATE OR SHORT-TERM STRATEGIES AT STRESS REDUCTION

Performance Appraisal

The current trend in performance appraisal is to move away from the *judgment* of a superior on the performance of a subordinate towards a *discussion* between colleagues about the progress of a job in which they both have an interest; one as the job holder and the other as being responsible for the performance of the job holder. Among others, Beveridge (1974) and Randell et al. (1972), have identified this trend and expounded its method. Personnel managers monitoring "performance review programs" and coaching managers in interview method could incorporate an element of stress identification in the procedures they advocate. Beveridge's approach is particularly susceptible to this type of development, because the job holder is encouraged to identify and comment upon the problems blocking effective performance. An interviewer with the requisite skill and sensitivity may enable the interviewee at least to engage in catharsis, with the possibility of going further by helping to work out adaptive behaviors for the job holder to initiate or to encourage stress-relieving initiatives within the organizational context in which the job is done.

The potential dangers of this approach are the temptation of the interviewer to play god—"Come unto me all ye who are heavy-laden and I will give you rest"—or seek out personal problems of the interviewee as a convenient reason for unsatisfactory performance, which neatly absolve the interviewer from taking any action or bearing any responsibility. Notwithstanding this hazard, the performance review still provides an opportunity for stress identification, because it is an occasion during which matters are being discussed in a manner more detached and reflective than in most interactive encounters at work.

Stress Counseling

An alternative may lie in the work of the small number of people employed in organizations in a quasiprofessional counseling capacity. Occasionally an organization will have in its ranks a professional psychologist, whose remit is to be available to discuss personal problems with employees. His/her services could be extremely helpful in providing a means towards stress-mitigation for individuals. The problem lies in the reluctance of the individual *to be seen* seeking such assistance, and it may be more effective if the expert masquerades under a title like Employee Relations or even Management Development Officer, whose advice could be sought without necessarily being seen as acknowledging a personal psychological impairment. A similar type of function could, however, be exercised by at least two other professionals who feature in some organizations: the doctor and the industrial chaplain, both of whom have the great advantage of being perceived as independent of the organization and its decision-making processes and thus as people not likely to weaken an employee's career prospects. Both are seen as appropriate repositories of confidences and as sources of two kinds of solace—medication or spiritual guidance—beyond the capacity of the organization.

A British Institute of Management survey (BIM, 1971) indicated that only 5 percent of companies have health care schemes which included psychiatric counseling as part of the scheme, but this referred only to organizations actually employing a psychiatrist specifically for this purpose. The survey concluded:

> . . . if one believes that managers need health care primarily because of the stress of their work, then this would be a useful adjunct to a normal check-up, and many doctors do include this as part of the regular medical check-up.

If counseling on stress is available from the doctor on demand, then it may well produce the type of inhibition already described for other possible initiatives, but an established practice of regular health checks on employees sets up a cycle of encounters in which there is the possibility of stress being discussed. There are the additional obvious advantages that the doctor will be able to diagnose a wider range of stress symptoms than other potential interveners, as well as be able to infer stress-proneness from a medical history. It is beyond our competence to consider the place of medication in mitigating stress, but if it is appropriate, only the doctor, within the organization, can provide it. There is, however, an encouraging pharmacological advance in beta-adrenergic blockers which may help to prevent or delay stress manifestations, especially ischaemic heart disease and, possibly, hypertension.

The BIM survey also showed there to be over 600 full-time company doctors and 1,000 part-time doctors in 1971 in the U.K. Prentice (1976) calculates that there were 150 full-time industrial chaplains and 450 part-time chaplains in 1976, so that they are numerically fewer than others. This is because there has been no ecclesiastical equivalent of the U.K. Health and Safety at Work Act to boost the number of chaplains and their services are not as universally acceptable as those of the doctors. It also appears that their activities are mainly directed towards the needs of shop-floor workers rather than managers. Nevertheless, they are perceived as being neutral and they carry out their duties principally by walking around and talking to people without arousing too much suspicion about their motives. Like the doctor, their training and vocation has familiarized them with the counseling role and the revelation of people's deep fears and anxieties. Here, potentially, is another source of external intervention.

Stress Awareness Training

A third area of operations, usually under the control of the personnel specialists, is training, and again, there are stress-relieving possibilities. The purpose of training courses is to aid the operational performance of course attenders when they return to their normal work role and, if the course succeeds in this, it is likely to reduce stress-proneness by increasing the feeling of competence and confidence that the trainee has in relation to his work. Also, the course extracts a person from his normal work environment for a period in which he is relieved of the normal pressures of his duties, with the opportunity to reflect upon them, discuss them with others, and potentially set them in a more healthy perspective. Both of these features are built in to almost any course.

Certain features of training could be considered to deal with stress symptoms more directly. The first is experiential learning techniques such as sensitivity training, which enables people to see themselves as others see them, by stripping away cultural inhibitions about self-presentation and self-awareness (Cooper, 1979). This can help a person to a more realistic perception of himself, and possibly, help him to better cope with some of his stresses. This is a method of training that has been criticized because of its potential *stressfulness* for some people (Cooper, 1975), and it may seem strange that it is advocated as a means of stress mitigation, but it is another feature of the overall dilemma already mentioned: what may be stressful for one person may be stress-relieving for another. Secondly, the course could include training in methods of slowing down the physiological processes, such as yoga or Transcendental Meditation, which we discussed in detail earlier. No doubt this will be regarded as an absurd suggestion by many industrial trainers, who would envisage the incredulity and resentment of some course attenders to the suggestion that such techniques could have an appropriate place in industrial training. Nevertheless, it has been demonstrated that these are methods that succeed in enabling people to relax. For that reason they have a potential place in management training. The third possibility is probably the easiest, and this is to include in a course some focus on, or discussion of, stress at work. This would at least succeed in bringing the issue out into the open and moderating the degree of shame that course members may feel in acknowledging their own stress-proneness.

Lessening Organizational Dependency

If an individual employee is overly dependent on his employing organization, there are a number of disadvantages: he is likely to become overcautious, anxious, reluctant, and generally view his compliance to the employment contract as being obligatory rather than volitional. Coincidentally, it may make him more susceptible to stress as the anticipated whims and vagaries of superiors assume alarming significance.

In the late seventies, we have a worldwide situation in which many employees feel very dependent on their current employer because of the sluggishness of the job market. Other jobs are difficult to find and the numbers of jobless continue to rise. Although personnel specialists may not be able to influence the external job market, there are other opportunities to heighten job security by reducing organizational dependence.

One strategy, in which we may be seen to have a vested interest, is to give better opportunities for improving professional qualifications. Studies like that of Page (1976), show the relative difficulty of obtaining reemployment among those in executive positions whose skills and experience have been specific to one organization. When no longer required in that context, a period of retraining is necessary to find employment elsewhere. Allied to this is the more general problem of skill obsolescence, as some specializations become less important in organizational life (Cooper, 1979). Enabling employees to enhance their general employability can increase their sense of job security by increasing the range of options they see before them. It has already been suggested in this chapter that the purpose of training is to aid the operational performance of those attending courses. If this is achieved by in-company training only, the range of skills and knowledge will be oriented towards those requisite within the organization. Provision of day- and block-release for externally moderated qualifications, like professional-body diplomas and university masters programs, can provide people with a wider range of enhanced capacities as well as "a piece of paper" with wider currency, avoiding the claustrophobia felt by many employees who see their skills as irrelevant outside their own organization. It is presumably a narrow and outdated view to criticize such opportunities on the grounds that a prized member of the organization is more likely to leave.

A further possibility is to review personnel policy on fringe benefits. It seems particularly pertinent to mention this at a time when there are many rumors, and some evidence, that companies are seeking to extend fringe benefits for employees (as compensation for being constrained by direct or indirect "income policy") in adjusting salaries. Common executive benefits, like the company car, assisted house purchase, and subsidized lunches, can make people organizationally dependent by reducing the freedom of movement of those enjoying the benefits. It would be unrealistic to suggest that such benefits should be removed, but their extension needs very careful consideration.

One of the main determinants of organizational dependency is, of course, the pension arrangement. Until now most private sector pension schemes have provided relatively attractive pensions to the managerial elite, but with the penalty of nontransferability or limited transferability. The new state pension scheme which came into effect in April, 1978 in the United Kingdom, for example, provides stronger competition for the private pensions industry, but there remains a range of options to employers within the state framework. Existing private pension schemes can be wound up, employees can be contracted out of the additional pension element of the state scheme, or state and private arrangements can be integrated. Many of these decisions have still to be taken, and we suggest that one question for personnel practitioners to ask is: Which arrangement will lessen organizational dependency?

Clarity of Promotion Criteria

The personnel literature is replete with advice on career development and complaints about its scarcity. Glueck (1974) echoes the common cry:

> Unfortunately, most organizations are not at present concerned with career development. They would not think of ignoring financial planning or materials replacement planning, but the human resource is likely to deteriorate or fail to be used well without career development plans.

The considerable, if short-lived, popularity of M.B.O. was based on the simple proposition that performance was improved if people knew what they had to do and how they were getting on. We suggest here that this same simple proposition may be a way of reducing individual stress. It is axiomatic that the majority of people in executive positions are seeking advancement to a post of greater authority, scope, or financial remuneration; if this were not so they would not put their foot on the first rung of the ladder. Yet how often do they know the performance criteria for advancement? Career development programs that we have seen are unusually highly specific for junior positions, with a progressive decline in clarity as the program moves up the hierarchy. The problem is a dual one. First, a program of career development implies that the person who achieves the declared objectives will reap the benefit, and if, for instance, five people meet the outline requirement to be the next marketing manager, only one of them will be successful, and even that depends on the present incumbent's deciding to leave or retire. Secondly, the career development program may be suspect in the face of change. Criteria set out in 1980 may have become irrelevant in 1982.

Despite the difficulties, there usually are ways in which the future can be made clearer and more comprehensible for people; and a realistic increase in clarity can help to moderate individual stress.

Self-Analysis Drills

The last of our operational suggestions is quite an original one. Whereas we have so far been considering possible developments in operations already existing in most organizations, this potential initiative is the provision of a self-analysis aid, whereby an individual can carry out his own diagnosis of his own behavior in order to determine whether he is under stress or not. Symptom awareness training is one example of this, and many occupational health specialists argue that this is the first step in stress prevention. Some company doctors would go further and suggest that this is all that is needed, since the successful management of stress must ultimately rely on the individual's own initiative once he has been made aware of his own stress-related behavior. Not much has been done to implement this type of training in industry but model programs are available from the mental health field (Cooper and Payne, 1980). An example of a questionnaire that could help individuals become aware of their stress symptoms was designed by Gurin and is shown on pages 164–65.) It has been adapted by the author for use by a European, as well as American, audience.

INFLUENTIAL: POLICY AND LONG-TERM STRESS PREVENTION

Industrial Democracy and the Managerial Role

Moving now to our second category we begin to consider those initiatives related to personnel influence in organizations rather than personnel operations, and the first suggestion is

SYMPTOMS OF STRESS QUESTIONNAIRE

Below is a list of different troubles and complaints which people often have. For each one please tick the column which tells how often you have felt like this during the last three months.

		I feel like this:			
		A lot	Quite often	Occasionally	Never
1.	Do you ever have any trouble getting to sleep or staying asleep?	___	___	___	___
2.	Have you ever been bothered by nervousness, feeling fidgety or tense?	___	___	___	___
3.	Are you ever troubled by headaches or pains in the head?	___	___	___	___
4.	Are there any times when you just don't feel like eating?	___	___	___	___
5.	Are there times when you get tired very easily?	___	___	___	___
6.	How often are you bothered by having an upset stomach?	___	___	___	___
7.	Do you find it difficult to get up in the morning?	___	___	___	___
8.	Does ill-health ever affect the amount of work you do?	___	___	___	___
9.	Are you ever bothered by shortness of breath when you are not exercising or working hard?	___	___	___	___
10.	Do you ever feel 'put out' if something unexpected happens?	___	___	___	___
11.	Are there times when you tend to cry easily?	___	___	___	___
12.	Have you ever been bothered by your heart beating hard?	___	___	___	___
13.	Do you ever smoke, drink, or eat more than you should?	___	___	___	___

	A lot	Quite often	Occasionally	Never
14. Do you ever have spells of dizziness?	—	—	—	—
15. Are you ever bothered by nightmares?	—	—	—	—
16. Do your muscles ever tremble enough to bother you (e.g., hands tremble, eyes twitch)?	—	—	—	—
17. Do you ever feel mentally exhausted and have difficulty in concentrating or thinking clearly?	—	—	—	—
18. Are you troubled by your hands sweating so that you feel damp and clammy?	—	—	—	—
19. Have there ever been times when you couldn't take care of things because you just couldn't get going?	—	—	—	—
20. Do you ever just want to be left alone?	—	—	—	—

To the remaining questions please answer 'yes' or 'no'

	Yes	No
21. Do you feel you are bothered by all sorts of pains and ailments in different parts of your body?	————	————
22. For the most part do you feel healthy enough to carry out the things you would like to do?	————	————
23. Have you ever felt that you were going to have a nervous breakdown?	————	————
24. Do you have any particular physical or health problem?	————	————

Source: Slightly adapted version of Gurin's Psychosomatic Symptom List, in G. Gurin, J. Veroff, and S. Feld, *Americans View Their Mental Health* (New York: Basic Books, 1960).

concerned with industrial democracy and the role of managers within that type of structure.

Weir (1976) has recently given sharp focus to the widely held belief that managers are apprehensive about the development of union involvement in the management of companies, even when the managers are unior members themselves. He surveyed the attitudes of 1,147 managers in a large, profitable U.K. organization in the food and drink industry that had a good reputation for employee relations and is regarded as having an overt commitment to progressive personnel policies. Forty-five percent of them felt that, they, as a category of employee, were "looked after" worse than in the past and that manual workers had more direct and comprehensive access to top management than they had themselves. Later he demonstrates that there is a feeling among his respondents that employees should have a greater say in running the company, but this does not necessarily mean *union* involvement. Forty-seven percent of the union members (14 percent of the sample) were prepared to advocate more involvement by unions in management, but only 17 percent of nonunionists.

The general trend towards industrial democracy (particularly in Europe) is a source of anxiety to managers, producing problems about self-esteem and considerable role ambiguity. Strategies to deal with this are easy to see, but less easy to implement. The obvious initiative is to involve managers in consultation and decision making to the extent they regard as desirable—76 percent of Weir's respondents felt that they were not sufficiently consulted about matters which directly affected them. The obstacles are considerable. First, they are likely to lack the machinery and "will" to find and accept a common representative figure, because of the diversity of their interests and their concomitant disinterest in unionism. Second, other employees may regard consultation by management with managers as "the opposing high command consulting with the supplies officers before launching the attack." Third, what managers seek from consultation may frequently be the maintenance of an extension of a series of differential gaps between themselves and "other employees."

The strategy which we hope personnel specialists may be able to adopt in this connection is to whittle down the traditional managerial view of status and self-esteem, being seen in terms of hierarchical position and the number of subordinates. If managers can gradually adjust their sights to see their status in terms of "contribution" to the organization instead of "place" in the organization's hierarchical structure, then the stressful potential of industrial democracy and its evolution will be reduced and the potential value of such evolution will itself be enhanced. To achieve such a change will depend on some of the strategies already discussed, such as performance appraisal and training, and will inevitably be influenced by remuneration policy. But the general contribution of personnel specialists to the development of thinking and employment *policy,* within their companies, is another potential influence.

The Nature of Managerial Jobs

There is a tendency to believe that manual, and some clerical, employees have jobs that are routine and lacking in intrinsic motivations. We need also to realize that some managerial jobs are also of this type. Campbell et al. (1970) surveyed thirty-nine United States organizations with a high reputation for the development of managerial talent and concluded:

Management was characterized by having rather narrow jobs and very tightly written job descriptions that almost seemed designed to take the newness, conflict and challenge out of the job.

The current interest in the quality of working life generally appears to assume that managerial life already has quality and that it is only the nonmanager's working life that needs moderation. The irony is that so many studies and other indicators, like managerial membership of trade unions, indicate a growing disenchantment, with many managers failing to find in their work those intrinsic motivations that we are so busily trying to inject into the lives of those engaged in demonstrably prosaic work. The reasons for this are well documented, with specialization, technology, organization size, and degree of bureaucratization being the most common, together with resentment of apparent union influence that we have already considered. We should add to this a particular version of the problem of specialization, and that is the growth in the number of specialists, each of whom reduce the wholeness of the job done by someone else. For years this has been seen as the particular problem of the foreman, who has seen his autonomy gradually reduced by the arrival of the work study specialist, the production controller, the industrial relations officer, etc. More senior managers have not perhaps acknowledged and come to terms with the extent to which the specialists are reducing the wholeness of their jobs as well.

Out of the immense and ever-expanding literature on motivation and job satisfaction, we can pick the work of Hackman and Lawler (1971) who demonstrated the crucial importance of the scope for making a significant contribution to the total task in considering the sources of "achievement feelings" in individuals at work. Personnel officers should ask themselves to what extent they now are reducing the contribution of other managers, and so removing a key element from the jobs of their managerial colleagues. Personnel specialists have long cast themselves in the role of "John the Baptist," crying aloud in a wilderness of managerial indifference. Influential and well-informed figures in the personnel management world now aver that those days are past and the reasons are evident: legislation, incomes policy, the need for collective bargaining, the growth of union membership, and the decline of employee deference being at the top of the list. The personnel specialists move to the center of the stage, acquiring the status, power, money, and limelight he has always craved; but his gain is another's loss because the advisory role becomes a control function to achieve consistency, and changes to increase consistency involve reducing discretion and flexibility available to managers. The difficult question here for personnel specialists, in their influencing, is how can managerial jobs gain features to replace the discretion that the specialists remove?

Selection and Promotion Criteria

Change of function within the organization, as well as joining a new one, is a time of stress for the individual. Conventionally, such changes of function are promotions or carry some other benefit to make the change attractive, so there is useful enthusiasm and commitment to counter the stress hazard. But apart from the normal "settling in" problems of a new job, there is the question of whether the selection/promotion decision has been soundly based, so that the promotee is being drawn into a new role with which he can cope. The danger is that the Peter Principle will operate and the promotee will find that he has reached the level of his own incompetence resulting in his remaining in that stressful situation because he is not able to display efficient competence to be promoted out of it. The conventional method of avoiding such an error is to exhort the decision makers to pay close attention to the fullness of the job description and to their selection criteria. Equally conventional, however, is the detailed job description and personnel specification that focuses on the specialist aspects of the job and guesses about the personal attributes of candidates that will equip them for those specialized tasks. Seldom is this approach effective in telling us what *skills* are called for.

A recent advance achieved through the work of Rosemary Stewart (1976) may help in improving the effectiveness of job analysis for selection and placement and in attempting to provide generic classifications of management jobs. After analyzing some 450 managerial jobs, she produced a typology based mainly on the nature of the contacts that the job required, since this was regarded as the main differentiation between them. A total of twelve jobs are in four groups: *Hub, Peer Dependent, Man Management,* and *Solo.* These terms partly explain themselves, but it is necessary to read the text to see the extent to which this typology succeeds in extending simple common sense ideas about the demands of jobs, by drawing in the degree of contacts which job holders have to make inside and outside the organization, the level at which they make internal contacts, the nature of their relationship with the people they contact, the importance of cooperation, the time spent in contact, the significance of bargaining and of risk taking, and other factors which give credence to the typology and thus make it possible to construct job profiles and to provide a visual means of comparing the demands of the job a person is in with the demands of a job he might move into.

This provides the opportunity to draw up job descriptions and specifications with an additional dimension relating to the demands of a job, and then shows how the job profile could be used to describe the demands, constraints, and choices in a job in such a way that requisite skills can also be described. It would be naive of us to suggest that this would prevent the promotion of people who are not appropriately qualified. The aspiration of individuals is seldom sufficiently rational for them to accept that a particular promotion would not suit them, in spite of the fact that it pays X dollars a year more than their present post; and those making appointments may not have a field from which to choose. Despite this the Stewart job profile method might prevent some stressful promotions and would, at least, succeed in describing the demands, constraints, and choices of a new job in enough detail for a promotee to go into a new situation with his eyes open.

Grievance Procedures

There is little evidence recently available on the issues now being processed through grievance channels in organizations, but what is clear is that every employee of an organization, including managers, must be advised of the "grievance resolution channel" personally available to him. Although this is traditionally the domain of the shop steward taking up the case of an aggrieved manual employee, there is now the possibility of more individuals using this procedure as a way of seeking satisfaction of complaints. We have earlier argued that the main problem of the stressed manager is the difficulty he has in acknowledging that he is under stress in the first place. Therefore, it is not likely that he will make a complaint that he is being stressed, but it may still be useful for the personnel specialist to monitor grievances in procedure as a possible stress indicator. Roethlisberger and Dickson (1939) made the simple and profound observation forty years ago that complaints involving the hopes and fears of employees had both a *manifest* and a *latent* content—one thing was said, but much more was meant. If an organization has managers personally using grievance procedures—which seem unlikely—a "pull" on that particular communication cord can be a cue to the personnel specialist of a stressful situation. It is more likely that grievances coming from other people in the area, for which the manager is responsible, may have a latent content indicating that the manager is showing stress symptoms in his dealings with subordinates.

Job Mobility

One very specific source of stress is the need for employees to move to other regions of the country. In certain large companies and public sector organizations this is a well-established aspect of personnel policy. Promotion accompanies movement. In this situation the translated manager has the usual problems of a new job plus the domestic and family problems that relocation brings, as discussed in the last chapter. We suggest that relocation problems are increasing rather than lessening. The direct and indirect financial commitment in buying and selling houses is generally regarded as getting greater, and parents frequently feel that the standard of public schools varies so considerably that a geographical move could disadvantage children to a greater extent than moving between private schools. Most significantly of all new factors in the mobility argument is the attitude and earning potential of the wife. We do not suggest that all mobile employees are men, but the very great majority are married men. If the wife is content to be a housewife she has to cope with the loneliness of settling in a new town, while her husband "escapes" to work with its built-in social contacts. If she is not content with being a housewife, there are a variety of developments which influence her mobility. Twenty percent of households now have the wife as the principal earner. Presumably few of these are at the earnings level of the conventional mobile manager, but at a time of incomes policy and inflation, the significance of the wife's income is considerable and not to be jeopardized. Also, some of the jobs popular among the wives of mobile managers are less readily transferable than they were. The prime example is schoolteaching, where the numbers of unemployed school teachers make it unlikely that a woman can uproot from one town to another and readily find a teaching post, even though this was commonplace until the middle seventies.

The research of Birch and Macmillan (1971) gives some indication of the scale, for example, of managerial mobility. Examining the period up to 1970, they found that the average number of regional moves per manager of 0.7 in 1940 had more than doubled to an average of 1.6 in 1970, with 15 percent of managers moving four or more times in their careers and university qualified managers moving more frequently than the average. Furthermore, in an in-depth study of mobile managers and their wives, Marshall and Cooper (1976) found that the stresses on the managers and their families during and after a relocation were greater and more complex than anticipated. They concluded that much of the stress and manager's ability to cope depended on the stage of their life cycle (e.g., single, married with no children, married with young children, married with older children or empty nest, as discussed in Chapter 7). Unfortunately many managers are relocated at the most inappropriate life stage for the family, that is, when the manager has young, school-aged children and a "captive wife."

The question we raise here is to ask how necessary is the policy of some organizations in explicitly or implicitly making "willingness to move" a condition of promotion. Many people will seek geographical relocation at some time in their careers, but if people are not able to determine when and where they move, but have to accept the move when it is offered or slip several prospective rungs on the promotion ladder, then they become candidates for stress because of family-company interface conflict. We believe that the widespread convention of linking promotion with geographical relocation could benefit from reappraisal.

Further Considerations

Having presented our ten possible initiatives, we mention some of the long-range features of working organizations that are stressful, but solutions to which are difficult to see. If, however, they can be discussed, solutions may emerge, even though they seem intractable at the moment.

First we ask the question about movement in the hierarchy. Moving up the hierarchy is generally attractive; moving down is unthinkable. How can we learn to find a move down the hierarchy as attractive as a move up? Perhaps this is beyond the capacity of those of us who spend our working lives in organizations, but if such moves ever become attractive we can see solutions to some of the stressful predicaments of those employees who have outlived their usefulness in a particular position, yet who hang on grimly to avoid the nightmarish situation of losing face. Closely linked with this is our second question: Does the organization always have to be a hierarchy with the greatest rewards and prerequisites automatically going to the top? Is there any possibility of an organization succeeding in which the position of chief executive is just a job like any other? One of the inferences of Stewart's (1976) recent work and Cooper and Marshall's (1978) study described earlier is that many hierarchically middle- and junior-range positions are more stressful than those of more senior officeholders, even though the reward system does not usually acknowledge this.

What the Individual Can Do to Cope with Work Pressures
chapter 9

The Coping Process

Stress at work is a result of the interaction between the individual and his work environment. To better understand what the individual can do to meet these pressures, it is necessary to examine the *coping process* itself (see Figure 9.1).

Initially, a particular combination of pressures is "identified" as stressful by the individual—he feels anxious, unable to cope, and displays his characteristic pattern of physical and mental symptoms of stress and defensive behavior. This is the period of "shock," described by Lazarus (1967) in his four-stage model of stress, during which the individual builds up strength to face the future. The behavior which follows this period of "protective withdrawal" can be categorized as either adaptive or maladaptive depending on the consequences it has for the individual concerned (and subsequently his colleagues, organization, family, etc.). Adaptive behavior deals directly with the stressful situation by seeking and implementing solutions; it not

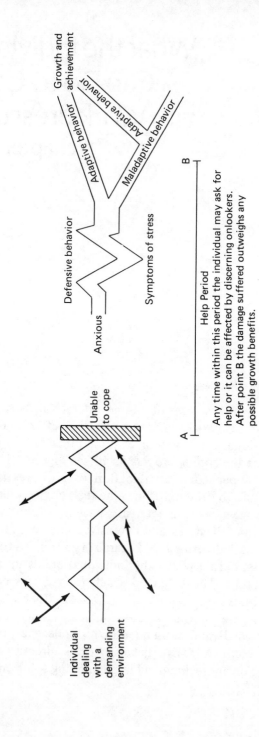

Individual dealing with a demanding environment

Unable to cope

Anxious

Defensive behavior

Symptoms of stress

Adaptive behavior

Growth and achievement

Adaptive behavior

Maladaptive behavior

A

B

Help Period

Any time within this period the individual may ask for help or it can be affected by discerning onlookers. After point B the damage suffered outweighs any possible growth benefits.

FIGURE 9.1 The Coping Process

Source: C.L. Cooper and J. Marshall, "The Management of Stress," *Personnel Review*, Autumn 1975.

only does away with the current problems but also prepares the individual to deal with similar situations in the future, and can lead to a well-earned sense of achievement. Adaptive behavior is, therefore, developmental. Maladaptive behavior, on the other hand, does not deal directly with the problem; it is self-protective, and while it may remove the stress situation, it is not likely to do so temporarily. It frequently does not dissipate the anxiety felt by the individual and does not help him to cope with future similar situations. In Figure 9.1 it is suggested that maladaptive behavior can profitably become adaptive any time up to Point B, after which the negative consequences (psychological distress, disruption of work performance and relationships, etc.) cannot be compensated for by the possible benefits of ultimate successful coping. The management of stress should be concerned with how this switch (from maladaptive to adaptive behavior) can be achieved, who should be involved, and what actions are appropriate.

An example of the dynamics of the stress/coping process can be seen in respect to a typical executive in an industrial organization. He or she deals actively with the internal and external environment, both receiving and making demands. Then (Point A) a particular configuration of demands (say, an ambiguously worded request from the boss), coming in a particular situation (already overloaded with work), is perceived by this particular individual (who fears being seen as incompetent) as stressful. His/her immediate defensive behavior might well be to accept the request without question even though he doesn't understand it (thus not admitting weakness), or to put it aside for a day or two (to delay recognizing the fact that he doesn't understand it), or to avoid the boss.

An adaptive sequel to this would be to return fairly soon to the boss, ask some considered and pertinent questions, and arrive at an understanding of what has been asked for. By so doing the individual will: (1) know what is required; (2) have improved the relationship with his boss and, thus, reduced the likelihood of similar incidents happening in the future; and (3) (normally) not have damaged his reputation with him.

When should intervention take place? In Figure 9.1, we have designated a "help period" ending at Point B. Up to this point the damage caused to any of the parties is minimal; the psychological tension felt by the individual concerned is likely to be an impetus to, and a necessary precondition of, growth and achievement. It is only if maladaptive behavior follows Point B that permanent damage becomes a probability; it is here, therefore, that "intervention" is appropriate. Intervention is used to mean initiative to treat the situation as a problem rather than to pretend that it is manageable within already established work routines. This initiative may come from one of three groups, which can be distinguished in terms of both the directness of their relationship with the problem situation and also their ability to intervene effectively. At the focus of the situation is the *individual concerned*—only he has full information regarding what the sources of stress are (having defined them as such himself). The most immediate and effective action can be expected if he/she asks for help. If, however, the individual concerned avoids admitting his/her feelings, it may be necessary for someone close to them to recognize the situation and to take action. These are people who relate directly to the individual—*the boss, colleagues, wife/husband*—and who thus should have some idea as to what his overall circumstances are and how he/she is coping with them. In many cases the problem is not, in fact, dealt with until members of the third group of people, *outsiders,* have become involved—company doctors, counselors, or higher level managers to whose attention unsatisfactory work, poor health, etc., has been brought.

It is best, for many reasons, if the initiative comes from the individual under stress, for the action is more immediate, loss of self-esteem is less likely, and the situation is not likely to have developed to an unmanageable stage. The *management of stress* should be concerned with making this outcome the most likely.

A necessary prerequisite to answering the question "How

can this be done?" is to understand why so many people suffer stress in comparative silence. There are two fundamental reasons for this: (1) lack of awareness by the individual as to the exact nature or source of his/her stress at work; and (2) the fear of sanctions—from the company, colleagues, and boss—if he/she admits to an inability to cope. In terms of this latter point, most companies still operate a "survival of the fittest" mentality: "If you can't cope, get out." Employees are very reluctant to admit their vulnerability or even to discuss it at work, for fear of the consequences for their career development and job security. It will be the task of work organizations over the next decade, with prompting by occupational safety and health authorities, and more humane societal norms generally about the quality of worklife, to help create an organizational atmosphere and structure in which employees will feel free to express their inability to cope, to discuss their fears and concerns, and to be able to ask for help.

As far as the first point is concerned, it is very important for employees to be more aware of the characteristics of their work situation that may be responsible for their dissatisfaction and/or stress at work.

Assessing Your Own Organizational Work Pressures

Before an individual can begin to deal with work-related sources of stress, one must be able to identify them. The two questionnaires which follow should help anyone who may have these sorts of pressure at work. They both focus on those potentially stressful aspects of the work environment which were discussed at the beginning of Chapter 8: characteristics intrinsic to the nature of the job; role clarity, ambiguity, and conflict; relationships at work; career development; organizational structure and climate; and home-work interface conflicts.

After an individual has diagnosed the main stressors in the

COOPER'S JOB STRESS QUESTIONNAIRE

Could you please circle the number that best reflects the degree to which the particular statement is a source of stress for you at work?

	No stress at all					A great deal of stress
			STRESS			
My relationship with my boss	0	1	2	3	4	5
My relationships with my colleagues	0	1	2	3	4	5
My relationships with my subordinates	0	1	2	3	4	5
Workload	0	1	2	3	4	5
Making mistakes	0	1	2	3	4	5
Feeling undervalued	0	1	2	3	4	5
Time pressures and deadlines	0	1	2	3	4	5
Promotion prospects	0	1	2	3	4	5
Rate of pay	0	1	2	3	4	5
Demands of work on my private life	0	1	2	3	4	5
My spouse's attitude towards my work	0	1	2	3	4	5
The amount of travel required by my work	0	1	2	3	4	5
Being relocated	0	1	2	3	4	5
Taking work home	0	1	2	3	4	5
Managing people	0	1	2	3	4	5
Office politics	0	1	2	3	4	5
Lack of power and influence	0	1	2	3	4	5
My beliefs conflicting with those of the company	0	1	2	3	4	5
Lack of consultation and communication in my company	0	1	2	3	4	5
Clarity of my job	0	1	2	3	4	5
Conflict between my work group and others in the organization	0	1	2	3	4	5
Top management does not understand my work-related problems	0	1	2	3	4	5

STRESSFUL WORK CONDITIONS

There frequently are day to day conditions at work which we find stressful. On the items below, indicate how often each source of stress is true for you by circling the appropriate number.

	Never	Rarely	Sometimes	Often	Always
1. Others I work with seem unclear about what my job is	1	2	3	4	5
2. I have differences of opinion with my superiors	1	2	3	4	5
3. Others' demands for my time at work are in conflict with each other	1	2	3	4	5
4. I lack confidence in "management"	1	2	3	4	5
5. "Management" expects me to interrupt my work for new priorities	1	2	3	4	5
6. There is conflict between my unit and others it must work with	1	2	3	4	5
7. I only get feedback when my performance is unsatisfactory	1	2	3	4	5
8. Decisions or changes which affect me are made "above" without my knowledge or involvement	1	2	3	4	5
9. I have too much to do and too little time to do it	1	2	3	4	5
10. I feel over qualified for the work I actually do	1	2	3	4	5
11. I feel under qualified for the work I actually do	1	2	3	4	5
12. The people I work closely with are trained in a different field than mine	1	2	3	4	5
13. I must go to other departments to get my job done	1	2	3	4	5
14. I have unsettled conflicts with people in my department	1	2	3	4	5
15. I have unsettled conflicts with other departments	1	2	3	4	5
16. I get little personal support from the people I work with	1	2	3	4	5
17. I spend my time "fighting fires" rather than working to a plan	1	2	3	4	5

	Never	Rarely	Sometimes	Often	Always
18. Management misunderstands the real needs of my department in the organization	1	2	3	4	5
19. I feel family pressure about long hours, weekend work, etc.	1	2	3	4	5
20. Self-imposed demand to meet scheduled deadlines	1	2	3	4	5
21. I have difficulty giving negative feedback to peers	1	2	3	4	5
22. I have difficulty giving negative feedback to subordinates	1	2	3	4	5
23. I have difficulty in dealing with aggressive people	1	2	3	4	5
24. I have difficulty dealing with passive people	1	2	3	4	5
25. Overlapping responsibilities cause me problems	1	2	3	4	5
26. I am uncomfortable arbitrating a conflict among my peers	1	2	3	4	5
27. I am uncomfortable arbitrating a conflict among my subordinates	1	2	3	4	5
28. Academic and administrative roles are in conflict	1	2	3	4	5
29. I avoid conflicts with peers	1	2	3	4	5
30. I avoid conflicts with superiors	1	2	3	4	5
31. I avoid conflicts with subordinates	1	2	3	4	5
32. Allocation of resources generates conflict in my organization	1	2	3	4	5
33. I experience frustration with conflicting procedures	1	2	3	4	5
34. My personal needs are in conflict with the organization	1	2	3	4	5
35. My professional expertise contradicts organizational practice	1	2	3	4	5
36. Administrative policies inhibit getting the job done	1	2	3	4	5
37. Other	1	2	3	4	5

Source: J. Steinmetz, "The stress reduction program at University Hospital, University of California Medical Center, San Diego," *Proceedings of the Conference on Occupational Stress,* sponsored by the National Institute of Occupational Safety and Health, November 1977, pp. 56-65.

work environment with the aid of these questionnaires or by other means, it is necessary to devise *personal action plans* to alleviate or cope with them, before they develop beyond Point B of the "helping period." These action plans must contain four essential ingredients. They must be: *realistic, legitimate* (within the context of the particular organization), *flexible* (in terms of objectives and timetables), and *progressive* (a gradual achievement of goals). Let's now examine each of the potential work stressors from the point of view of what individuals *themselves* can do to manage their own pressures.

Factors Intrinsic to the Job. Within this category of stressors there are a wide variety of job characteristics which can be a potential source of pressure. Some of these are amenable to change by individual action (through negotiation or careful planning), while others are outside his/her scope (e.g., work redesign).

Workload. Work overload can be a very serious pressure in any job. An individual is in an overload situation when he/she is assigned a large number of tasks to accomplish in an unreasonable time period (given a desired quality end product). This can cause excessive frustration and anxiety, and the deterioration of job satisfaction. In many cases, although management may be directly responsible for the timetabling, the individual has some scope for negotiation. Many people at work, however, are frightened to admit they can't do a particular job within a given time period set by their boss or higher level management. In this case, a self-fulfilling feedback loop is set in motion, where management continue to think the job can be done within the given time frame, and organize future work schedules accordingly. Unless the individual can confront his boss or some "significant other" with the difficulties he/she faces in meeting the deadlines, the problem will grow and everyone will lose. Individual *initiative* is needed in cases of work overload; it is not good enough to "grin and bear it," and then blame others for mismanagement, being inconsiderate or insensitive, and so on.

There are cases of self-imposed work overload as well. Some people create overload at work for a variety of different (and usually, unconscious) reasons: (1) to enhance their own status: "Having a full diary means I'm important," (2) to avoid doing certain aspects of their work they don't do well or don't like doing, or (3) to signal to others their indispensability, etc. It is important in this context that individuals be aware of the part they play in creating work overload, particularly if it is leading to personal or other work-related stress.

Work underload is also a potential stressor. It creates stress not only because these periods are boring and unproductive, but because they may make the individual feel less important or may signal to him/her (either accurately or paranoically) that others at work feel he is incapable of doing the job (thereby the low level of assigned work). In these circumstances, it is the individual's duty (to maintain his/her own well-being) to do some "reality testing," that is, to check with the boss and other colleagues about the nature of the current situation at work and the reasons for the shortfall. It may be that one of the individual's fantasies is accurate, in which case it is probably better to confront it. On the other hand, it may provide positive feedback to top management that the individual has spare capacity and, therefore, is capable of more demanding work.

Physical and Task Aspects of the Job.   More and more industrial organizations, as discussed earlier, are accepting work and job design innovations as part and parcel of the move to humanization of the workplace in American and European society. Individuals in organizations that have "works committees" or their equivalent at higher levels should take advantage of them. If they don't exist, one has the responsibility to see that consultation committees are established for purposes of making the job and physical environment at work more "satisfying" and challenging.

Increasing Role Clarity and Minimizing Role Ambiguity and Conflict. Stress is created at work (for some people) by the lack of clarity of their job role or the conflict it creates with other contiguous work roles (e.g., union or professional association representative). Role negotiation training is common with work groups who have had obvious difficulties, but very little has been done with particular individuals. In order to be successful in negotiating a change in one's work role, individuals must begin to take their own initiative and responsibility in this regard. I would like to suggest a possible approach in this respect:

> First, approach the person responsible for defining your role (e.g., boss, personnel manager) and discuss with him/her the problems you are experiencing. Suggest to them that you would like to have a more clear-cut agreement/understanding with them about the nature of your job, and that you would like to work jointly with them to this end.

Since most role problems are based on different expectations by the boss of the subordinate (and vice versa) or between colleagues, it is necessary for both parties to make clear which tasks, responsibilities, and behaviors are effective and which are ineffective in their working relationship. It is at this stage that it is important to build a negotiation contract with the relevant person(s), which will involve all the parties in the process of thinking (1) about the way work is conducted between them, (2) about what ways this could be changed for the better, (3) about what things should be kept the same or reduced or increased, and (4) about *who* and *what* would have to change in order to improve things (Harrison, 1972).

> Second, after establishing the principle of negotiating role clarity between yourself and the relevant other, arrange some time together. Then encourage your boss, colleague, client, etc., to provide three separate short lists of what he thinks (1) you should do *more of or better of,* (2) do *less of or stop doing,* and (3) *keep on doing,* or maintain unchanged in your job. In the meantime, you should

prepare the reverse list of what *you* think he should be doing (1) more of or better of, (2) less of or stop doing, and (3) keep on doing *in respect of you.*

Third, exchange your lists with one another. Each person is allowed to question the other(s) who have sent the message, focusing on the *what, why,* and *how* of their requests, but no one is allowed to defend themselves.

This is to ensure that each person has a clear understanding of the message of the other, and that both parties don't get trapped in defending their behavior, decisions, position, etc. As Harrison (1972) has suggested: "The strategy (of this sort of role negotiation exercise) is to channel the energy which has been generated or released by the sharing of demands and expectations into successful problem solving and mutual influence."

Fourth, important issues, tasks, behaviors should be selected for negotiation, so that future tasks, behaviors, and responsibilities can be agreed and will, hopefully, create less role ambiguity and conflict in the future. This must be done on a *quid pro quo* basis, that is, that both parties agree to change, otherwise the likelihood is that the same situation will recur again. The negotiation process should consist of each individual making "contingent offers to one another of the form, 'If you do *X,* I will do *Y*'." The negotiation ends when both parties are satisfied with the exchange for the particular issue, otherwise the process above is repeated until they are.

Improving Personal Relationships at Work. There are two potential problem areas in this respect. First, that a particular individual has difficulty in relating to others at work which stems more from his/her lack of social skills. Second, that the individual possesses adequate social skills but has difficulty with one or two specific colleagues, that is, a relationship-specific, as opposed to personality, problem. In the case of the first difficulty, a lack of interactive or social skills, individuals at work have a number of options open to them to improve and change their behavior. There are a wide variety of training courses available in the community (and in many cases, within organizations) to deal with human relations/social skills/interactive skills. The T-group or sensitivity training group, for example, is one such approach. This particular method, and many other experiential approaches to human relations training (which have burgeoned over the last two decades), rely on individuals learning about themselves by discovery, that is, by examining their own interpersonal behavior in the context of a group of peers, or work colleagues, or strangers with similar problems (Cooper, 1979). Indeed, *Newsweek* magazine wrote about the ever increasing use of these group exercises in the U.S. They described a one-night introduction to an encounter group in San Francisco's First Unitarian Church, in which 200 participants had paid five dollars to take part in a "relatively leaderless, structureless, agendaless "be in" intended to express human feelings and to cultivate close emotional ties between people." They went on to say that the human potential movement (e.g., encounter groups, T-groups, *gestalt* groups, etc.) "is involving Americans in their biggest emotional binge since V.J. Day"; and that, as Carl Rogers (1970) observed: "These groups are the most rapidly spreading phenomenon in the country." The article was entitled *The Group: Joy on Thursday* to illustrate that individuals now have available to them one-day opportunities of improving their personal and interpersonal relationships through a variety of group experiences.

In situations in which an individual has personality clashes with one or two specific colleagues at work, a similar negotiating procedure could be followed as discussed earlier. In this case, however, one would focus on the personal and interpersonal aspects of the relationship rather than on the tasks, responsibilities, etc. An alternative approach would be to discuss with the other person the fact that you feel unhappy about your relationship with him/her and that you would like to improve upon it. If the other person was agreeable, you might then arrange with your colleague to meet for a set period of time, and more systematically explore your relationship. Jones and Jones (1973) have designed a very progressive, interesting, and helpful set of questions you might want to work on, which they entitled *Dialog: A Program for Developing Work Relationships.* They say at the beginning of their program that "the basic purpose of the discussion which you are about to have is to foster greater understanding of each other at work. By telling about oneself and by sharing perceptions of each other you will be working toward a higher level of trust." The Dialog exercise consists of a series of open-ended statements, which each person responds to in turn. It starts off with less threatening statements such as: "Basically my job is . . . ; Usually I am the kind of person who . . . ; When things aren't going well I . . ."; etc. Then it develops more intimately, so that each person can share his perceptions of the other, with statements that each has to finish such as: "My first impression of you was . . . ; Your job seems to be . . . ; I usually react to negative criticism by . . . ; What I like about you is . . . ; What puzzles me about you is . . . ; Faced with a choice between the goals of the organization and your own welfare, I would predict that you would . . ."; etc. These statements build up gradually, allowing the individuals to systematically pursue their relationship and share information about one another that should help to create a better working relationship by providing each with a more realistic view of the other. It also attempts to encourage each person to *listen* more attentively to the other, by stopping them occasionally and suggesting: "During this discussion, you may wish to continue the development of your listening by using the phrase, 'What I hear you saying is . . .'."

Career Planning. In order to avoid the stressors associated with career development, it is important for the affected individual to begin to plan his long-term career prospects. Obviously something like the *life planning exercise* we discussed earlier can be of help in this regard. This could be extended to include one's boss or whoever else is responsible for the individual's career development. Many companies and public sector organizations have established procedures to engage in short-term career planning, but few look further into the future. The best strategy, therefore, seems to be one in which the individual concerned should first of all engage in a long-term career planning exercise based on the life planning approach and on his/her own. Next, he/she should devise family plans for the future, integrating them with their career plans, so that a total, integrated and mutually satisfying package emerges. After this process, the individual should discuss the finalized future career plans with the person responsible for his/her development. Only by making clear to others at work one's expectations, hopes, and goals can more realistic short-term planning be done by those responsible for career development in organizations.

Creating a More Open and Trusting Work Environment. Another major source of stress at work is the tendency of some organizations to be closed and untrusting, which leads to poor communications, lack of consultation, a climate of distrust among employees, maladaptive internal competition, and ultimately, to poorer performance and job dissatisfaction. It seems to me that this is an unnecessary destructive cyclical process which might be improved by greater organizational openness and honesty. The consequences of mistrust can, as Mellinger (1956) found in a large public research organization, lead to poor communications and ultimately to bad decision making.

(O = Organization, E = Employee):

O mistrusts → E	E consequently tends to conceal attitudes and information from O by communicating in ways that are: evasive, aggressive, misleading, etc.	→	O's perceptions of reality are consequently impaired, e.g., O in cases may overestimate agreement with E or O in cases may underestimate agreement with E

Ineffective communications and lack of trust lead us into another main source of stress—"poor relations within organizations." If we are to minimize the potential stress effects of "being in organizations," with all the behavioral restrictions that implies, and of poor relations between boss and subordinate, and between colleagues, organizations will have to consider change or development programs that will encourage trust-building activities. Organizational trust building is characterized by: (1) the development of a supportive organizational climate and norms, (2) the building of shared norms on the basis of perceived similarities in attitudes and experiences of people working in organizations, and (3) the development of "we-ness," a shared identity among workers that implies substantial common direction by all (Golembiewski and McConkie, 1975). More and more work is being carried out in the area of organizational change and development to create the conditions of trust and well-being within the workplace (Cooper, 1979) which should help to improve relations between boss and subordinate and between work colleagues, and help to make the constraints associated with living in an organization less stressful. As Bennis and Slater (1968) suggest in their book on the temporary society, "industrial life is so fast-moving and changeable that organizations have to adapt by being more flexible and by unfreezing their structures so that individuals are not locked into jobs that might put excessive stress on them." Burns and Stalker (1961) made this point in their book *The Management of Innovation* when they suggested that changing times demand more "organic" as opposed to "mechanistic" organizations.

The Management of Stress

Cooper and Marshall (1978) have argued that understanding the sources of organizational pressure, as we have tried to do in the last two chapters, is only the first step in stress reduction. Next, we must begin to explore when and how to intervene. There are a number of changes that can be introduced in organizational life to begin to manage stress at work, for example:

1. to recreate the social, psychological, and organizational environment in the work place to encourage greater autonomy and participation by people in *their* jobs

2. to begin to build the bridges between the work place and the home; providing opportunities for the employee's spouse to understand better the other's job, to express their views about the consequences of the other's work on family life, and to be involved in the decision-making process of work that affects all members of the family unit

3. to utilize the well-developed catalogue of social and interactive skill training programs to help clarify role and interpersonal relationship difficulties within organizations

4. and more fundamentally, to create an organizational climate to encourage rather than discourage communication, openness, and trust—so that individuals are able to express their inability to cope, their work-related fears, and are able to ask for help, if needed

There are many other methods and approaches of coping and managing stress, depending on the sources activated and the interface between these sources and the individual make-up of the person concerned. Nevertheless, one important point that must always be kept in mind in coping with and managing organizational stress is, as Wright (1975) so aptly summarizes, that "the responsibility for maintaining health should be a reflection of the basic relationship between the individual and the organization for which we works; it is in the best interests of both parties that reasonable steps are taken to live and work sensibly and not too demandingly."

References

CHAPTER 1

Aldridge, J.F.L., "Emotional Illness and the Working Environment," *Ergonomics,* 15 (5), 1970, 613-21.

Altman, I. and E. F. Lett, "The Ecology of Interpersonal Relationships: A Classification System and Conceptual Model," in J.E. McGrath (ed.) *Social and Psychological Factors in Stress.* New York: Holt, Rinehart and Winston, 1970, pp. 177-201.

Appley, M.H., "Motivation, Threat Perception and the Induction of Psychological Stress," *Proceedings of Sixteenth International Congress of Psychology.* Bonn: Amsterdam: North Holland, 1962, pp. 880-81.

Appley, M.H. and R. Trumbull, *Psychological Stress.* New York: Appleton, 1967.

Arnold, M., *Emotion and Personality,* vols. 1 and 2. New York: Columbia University Press, 1960.

Basowitz, H., H. Persky, S.J. Korchin and R.R. Grinker, *Anxiety and Stress.* New York: McGraw-Hill, 1955.

Bernard, J., "The Eudaemonists," in S.Z. Klausner (ed.) *Why Man Takes Chances.* New York: Garden City, 1968, pp. 6-47.

Brady, J.V., "Ulcers in 'Executive' Monkeys," in R.N. Haber, (ed.) *Current Research in Motivation.* New York: Holt, Rinehart and Winston, 1966, pp. 242-48.

Caplan, G., *Principles of Preventive Psychiatry.* London: Tavistock, 1964.

Carruthers, M.E., "Risk Factor Control," Paper presented to the conference 'Stress of the Air Traffic Control Officer (Latest Developments)'. Manchester: April, 1976.

Cofer, C.N. and M.H. Appley, *Motivation: Theory and Research.* New York: Wiley, 1964.

Corneille, P., *Le Cid,* in *Collins Gem Dictionary of Quotations.* London: Collins, 1976.

Dohrenwend, B.P., "The Social Psychological Nature of Stress: A Framework for Causal Inquiry," *Journal of Abnormal and Social Psychology,* 62 (2), 1961, 294-302.

Felton, J.S. and R. Cole, "The High Cost of Heart Disease." *Circulation,* 27, 1963, 957-62.

Froberg, J., C.G. Karlsson, L. Levi and L. Lidberg, "Physiological and Biochemical Stress Reactions Induced by Psychosocial Stimuli," in L. Levi (ed.) *Society, Stress and Disease,* vol. 1. London: Oxford University Press, 1971, pp. 280-98.

Gillespie, F., "Stress Costs More Than Strikes," *Financial Times,* April 26, 1974.

Hinkle, L.E., "The Concept of 'Stress' in the Biological and Social Sciences," *Science, Medicine and Man,* 1, 1973, 31-48.

Kahn, R.L., "Some Propositions Toward a Researchable Conceptualization of Stress," in J.E. McGrath (ed.) *Social and Psychological Factors in Stress.* New York: Holt, Rinehart and Winston, 1970, pp. 97-103.

Kenton, L., "Stress." *Unilever Magazine,* no. 9, 1974.

Lazarus, R.S., *Psychological Stress and the Coping Process.* New York: McGraw-Hill, 1966.

Lazarus, R.S., "Cognitive and Personality Factors Underlying Threat and Coping," in M.H. Appley and R. Trumbull, (eds.) *Psychological Stress.* New York: Appleton, 1967.

Lazarus, R.S., "The Concepts of Stress and Disease," in L. Levi (ed.) *Society, Stress and Disease,* vol. 1. London: Oxford University Press, 1971, pp. 53-60.

Leanderson, R. and L. Levi, "A New Approach to the Experimental Study of Stuttering and Stress," *Acta oto-laryng* (Stockholm) 311, Suppl. 224, 1976.

Lipawski, Z.J., "Psychosocial Aspects of Disease," *Annals of International Medicine*, 71, 1969, 1197-2006.

McGhee, L.C., "Psychological Signs of Executive Emotional Problems," *Industrial Medicine and Surgery*, 32 (5), 1963, 180-81.

McGrath, J.E., ed., *Social and Psychological Factors in Stress*. New York: Holt, Rinehart and Winston, 1970a.

McGrath, J.E., "A Conceptual Formulation for Research on Stress," in J.E. McGrath (ed.) *Social and Psychological Factors in Stress*. New York: Holt, Rinehart and Winston, 1970b.

Osler, W., "The Lumleian Lectures on *Angina Pectoris*," *The Lancet*, 1910, 696-700, 839-44, 974-77.

Pettigrew, A., "Managing Under Stress," *Management Today*, April, 1972.

Selye, H., "The General Adaptation Syndrome and the Diseases of Adaptation," *Journal of Clinical Endocrinology*, 6, 1946, 117.

Steiner, I.D., "Strategies for Controlling Stress in Interpersonal Situations," in J.E. McGrath (ed.) *Social and Psychological Factors in Stress*. New York: Holt, Rinehart and Winston, 1970, pp. 140-58.

Taylor, R., "Stress at Work," *New Society*, October 17, 1974.

Webber, R.A., "The Roots of Organizational Stress," *Personnel*, 43 (5), 1966.

Weick, K.E., "The 'Ess' in Stress: Some Conceptual and Methodological Problems," in J.E. McGrath (ed.) *Social and Psychological Factors in Stress*. New York: Holt, Rinehart and Winston, 1970, pp. 287-347.

Wright, H.B., *Executive Ease and Dis-ease*. Epping: Gower Press, 1975.

CHAPTER 2

Arnott, C.C., "Husbands' Attitude and Wives' Commitment to Employment," *Journal of Marriage and the Family*, 1972, 673-84.

Arnott, C.C., "Married Women and the Pursuit of Profit: An Exchange Theory Perspective," *Journal of Marriage and the Family*, 1977, 122-31.

Bakker, C.D., "Psychological Factors in *Angina Pectoris*," *Psychosomatic Medicine*, 8, 1967, 43-49.

Bebbington, A.C., "The Function of Stress in the Establishment of the Dual Career Family," *Journal of Marriage and the Family*, 1973, 530-37.

Bernard, J., *Academic Women*. University Park: The Pennsylvania State University Press, 1964.

Blood, R.O., "Long Range Causes and Consequences of the Employment of Married Women," *Journal of Marriage and the Family*, 1965, 43-47.

Blood, R.O. and R.L. Hamblin, "The Effect of the Wife Employment on the Family Power Structure," *Social Forces*, 1958, 347-52.

Bowman, G.W., N. Beatrice and S.A. Greyser, "Are Women Executives People?" *Harvard Business Review*, 1965, 14-17.

Breslow, L. and P. Buell, "Mortality from Coronary Heart Disease and Physical Activity of Work in California," *Journal of Chronic Diseases*, 11, 1960, 615-26.

Buck, V., *Working Under Pressure*. London: Staples Press, 1972.

Byre, S., "Nobody Home: the Erosion of the American Family, A Conversation with Urie Brofenbrenner," *Psychology Today*, May 1977.

Caplan, R.D., S. Cobb and J.R.P. French, "Relationships of Cessation of Smoking with Job Stress, Personality and Social Support," *Journal of Applied Psychology*, 60 (2), 1975, 211-19.

Caplan, R.D., S. Cobb, J.R.P. French, R. Van Harrison and S.R. Pinneau, "Job Demands and Worker Health: Main Effects and Occupational Differences," *Noish Research Report*, 1975.

Caplan, R.D. and K.W. Jones, "Effects of Workload, Role Ambiguity and Type A Personality on Anxiety, Depression and Heart Rate," *Journal of Applied Psychology*, 60, 1975, 713-19.

Chesney, M.A. and R.H. Rosenman, "Type A Behavior in the Work Setting," in C.L. Cooper and R. Payne (eds.) *Current Concerns in Occupational Stress*. London: John Wiley & Sons, 1980.

Cohen, L.M., "Women's Entry to the Professions in Columbia: Selected Characteristics," *Journal of Marriage and the Family*, 1973, vol. 19.

Constandse, W.J., "Mid-40s Man: A Neglected Personnel Problem," *Personnel Journal*, 51, 2, 1972, 129.

Cooper, C.L. and J. Marshall, "The Changing Roles of British Executives' Wives," *Management International Review*, 17, 1, 1977, 37-46.

Cussler, M., *The Woman Executive*. New York: Harcourt Brace, 1958.

Finn, F., N. Hickey and E.F. O'Doherty, "The Psychological Profiles of Male and Female Patients with CHD," *Irish Journal of Medical Science,* 2, 1969, 339-41.

French, J.R.P. and R.D. Caplan, "Psychosocial Factors in Coronary Heart Disease," *Industrial Medicine,* 39, 1970, 383-97.

French, J.R.P. and R.D. Caplan, "Organizational Stress and Individual Strain," in A. Marrow (ed.) *The Failure of Success.* New York: Amacom, 1973, pp. 30-66.

French, J.R.P., C.J. Tupper and E.I. Mueller, "Workload of University Professors," unpublished research report. Ann Arbor, Mich.: University of Michigan, 1965.

Friedman, M., *Pathogenesis of Coronary Artery Disease.* New York: McGraw-Hill, 1969.

Gavron, H., *The Captive Wife.* London: Routledge and Kegan Paul, 1966.

Ginzberg, E., *Life Styles of Educated Women.* New York: Columbia University Press, 1966.

Goffman, E., "On Cooling the Mark Out," *Psychiatry,* 15, 4, 1952, 451-63.

Gowler, D. and K. Legge, "Stress and External Relationships—the 'Hidden Contract'," in D. Gowler and K. Legge (eds.) *Managerial Stress.* Epping: Gower Press, 1975.

Heller, J., *Something Happened.* New York: Ballantine Books, 1975.

Hoffman, L.W., "Mother's Enjoyment of Work and Effects on the Child," in Hoffman and Nye (eds.) *The Employed Mother in America.* New York: Rand, 1963, pp. 95-105.

Jenkins, C.D., "Psychologic and Social Precursors of Coronary Disease," *New England Journal of Medicine,* 284, 5, 1971a, 244-55.

Jenkins, C.D., "Psychologic and Social Precursors of Coronary Disease," *New England Journal of Medicine,* 284, 6, 1971b, 307-17.

Kahn, R.L., D.M Wolfe, R.P. Quinn, J.E. Snoek and R.A. Rosenthal, *Organizational Stress.* New York: Wiley, 1964.

Kasl, S.V., "Mental Health and the Work Environment," *Journal of Occupational Medicine,* 15, 6, 1973, 509-18.

Kearns, J.L., *Stress In Industry.* London: Priory Press, 1973.

Kornhauser, A., *Mental Health of the Industrial Worker,* New York: Wiley, 1965.

Kritsikis, S.P., A.L. Heinemann and S. Eitner, "Die *Angina Pectoris* im Aspeckt Ihrer Korrelation mit Biologischer Disposition, Psychologischen und Soziologischem Emflussfaktoren," *Deutsch Gasundh,* 23, 1968, 1878–85.

Lazarus, R.S., *Psychological Stress and the Coping Process.* New York: McGraw-Hill, 1966.

Lebovits, B.Z., R.B. Shekelle and A.M. Ostfeld, "Prospective and Retrospective Studies of CHD," *Psychosomatic Medicine,* 19, 1967, 265–72.

Levinson, H., "Problems that Worry our Executives," in A.J. Marrow (ed.) *The Failure of Success.* New York: Amacom, 1973.

McMurray, R.N., "The Executive Neurosis," in R.L. Noland (ed.) *Industrial Mental Health and Employee Counseling.* New York: Behavioral Publications, 1973.

Marcson, S., *Automation, Alienation and Anomie.* New York: Harper and Row, 1970.

Margolis, B.L. and W.H. Kroes, "Work and the Health of Man," in J. O'Toole (ed.) *Work and the Quality of Life.* Cambridge, Mass.: MIT Press, 1974.

Margolis, B.L., W.H. Kroes and R.P. Quinn, "Job Stress: An Unlisted Occupational Hazard," *Journal of Occupational Medicine,* 16, 10, 1974, 654–61.

Martin, T.W., K.J. Berry and R.B. Jacobsen, "The Impact of Dual-Career Marriages on Female Professional Careers: an Empirical Test of a Parsonian Hypothesis," *Journal of Marriage and the Family,* 1975, 734–42.

Mettlin, C., "Occupational Careers and the Prevention of Coronary-Prone Behavior," *Social Science and Medicine,* 10, 1976, 367–72.

Mettlin, C. and J. Woelfel, "Interpersonal Influence and Symptoms of Stress," *Journal of Health and Social Behavior,* 15, 4, 1974, 311–19.

Orden, S. and B. Orden, "Working Wives and Marriage Happiness," *American Journal of Sociology,* vol. 74, 1969, 392–407.

Ostapen, L.V., "The Influence of the New Role of Women in Production on Their Position in the Family," *Ethnographic,* 1971, 95–102.

Paffenbarger, R.S., P.A. Wolf and J. Notkin, "Chronic Disease in Former College Students," *American Journal of Epidemiology,* 83, 1966, 314–28.

Pahl, R., "Review of Dual Career Families," *New Society,* vol. 19, 1971.

Pahl, J.M. and R.E. Pahl, *Managers and Their Wives.* London: Allen Lane, 1971.

Parsons, T., *Essays in Sociological Theory.* Glencoe, Illinois: The Free Press, 1954.

Payne, R., "A Type Work for A Type People?" *Personnel Management,* 7, 1975, 22-24.

Pincherle, G., "Fitness for Work," *Proceedings of the Royal Society of Medicine,* 65, 4, 1972, 321-24.

Powell, K.S., "Family Variables," in L. Hoffman and I. Nye (eds.) *The Employed Mother in America.* New York: Rand, 1963, 231-340.

Quinlan, C.B., J.G. Burrow and C.G. Hayes "The Association of Risk Factors and CHD in Trappist and Benedictine Monks," Paper presented to the American Heart Association, New Orleans, Louisiana, 1969.

Quinn, R.P., S. Seashore and I. Mangione, *Survey of Working Conditions.* US Government Printing Office, 1971.

Rapoport, R. and R. Rapoport, *Dual Career Families.* London: Penguin Books, 1971.

Rosenman, R.H., M. Friedman and C.D. Jenkins, "Clinically Unrecognized Myocardial Infarction in the Western Collaborative Group Study," *American Journal of Cardiology,* 19, 1967, 776-82.

Rosenman, R.H., M. Friedman and R. Strauss, "A Predictive Study of CHD," *Journal of the American Medical Association,* 189, 1964, 15-22.

Rosenman, R.H., M. Friedman and R. Strauss, "CHD in the Western Collaborative Group Study," *Journal of the American Medical Association,* 195, 1966, 86-92.

Russek, H.I. and B.L. Zohman, "Relative Significance of Hereditary, Diet and Occupational Stress in CHD of Young Adults," *American Journal of Medical Science,* 235, 1958, 266-75.

Sales, S.M., "Differences Among Individuals in Affective, Behavioral, Biochemical, and Physiological Responses to Variations in Work Load," doctoral dissertation, The University of Michigan, Ann Arbor, Mich.: University Microfilms No. 60-18098, 1969.

Shepard, J.M., *Automation and Alienation.* Cambridge, Mass.: MIT Press, 1971.

Shirom, A., D. Eden, S. Silberwasser and J.J. Kellerman, "Job Stresses and Risk Factors in Coronary Heart Disease Among Occupational Categories in Kibbutzim," *Social Science and Medicine,* 7, 1973, 875-92.

Siegel, A.E., and others, "Dependence and Independence in Children," in L. Hoffman and I. Nye (eds.) *The Employed Mother in America*. New York: Rand, 1963, 67–81.

Sleeper, R.D., "Labor Mobility Over the Life Cycle," *British Journal of Industrial Relations*, XIII, 2, 1975.

Sofer, C., Men in Mid-Career. Cambridge University Press, 1970.

Staines, G.L., J.H. Pleck, L. Shepard and P. O'Connor, "Wives' Employment Status and Marital Adjustment," unpublished manuscript, Institute for Social Research, University of Michigan, 1979.

Tropman, J.E., "The Married Professional Social Worker," *Journal of Marriage and the Family*, 1968, 661–65.

Waldron, I., A. Hickey, C. McPherson, and others, "Relationships of the Coronary Prone Behavior Pattern to Blood Pressure Variation, Psychological Characteristics, and Academic and Social Activities of Students," unpublished manuscript, University of Pennsylvania, 1978.

Wardwell, W.I., M. Hyman and C.B. Bahnson, "Stress and Coronary Disease in Three Field Studies," *Journal of Chronic Diseases*, 17, 1964, 73–84.

Wright, H.B., *Executive Ease and Dis-ease*. Epping: Gower Press, 1975.

Zajur, N.Y. and E. Ocio, "Leisure Work and the Women," *Revista Espanole de la Opinion Publica*, 1972, 251–97.

CHAPTER 3

Appley, M.H., "On the Concept of Psychological Stress," paper presented at the *Psychology Colloquim*, State University of New York, Buffalo, December, 1964.

Caplan, R.D., S. Cobb, J.R.P. French, R. Van Harrison and S.R. Pinneau, "Job Demands and Worker Health: Main Effects and Occupational Differences," *NIOSH Research Report*, 1975.

Cherry, N., "Stress, Anxiety and Work: Longitudinal Study," *Journal of Occupational Psychology*, 51, 1978, 259–70.

Conley, R.W., M. Conwell and M.B. Arill, "An Approach to Measuring the Cost of Mental Illness," in R.L. Noland (ed.) *Industrial Mental Health and Employee Counseling*. New York: Behavioral Publications, 1973.

Cooper, C.L. and R. Payne, *Stress at Work*. London: John Wiley & Sons, 1978.

Felton, J.S. and R. Cole, "The High Cost of Heart Disease," *Circulation,* 27, 1963, 957-62.

Gillespie, F., "Stress Costs More Than Strikes," *Financial Times,* April 26, 1974.

Heller, J., *Something Happened*. New York: Ballantine Books, 1975.

Hinkle, L.E., "The Concept of 'Stress' in the Biological and Social Sciences," *Science, Medicine and Man,* 1, 1973, 31-48.

McGrath, J.E., *Social and Psychological Factors in Stress*. New York: Holt, Rinehart and Winston, 1970.

McMurray, R.N., "The Executive Neurosis," in R.L. Noland (ed.) *Industrial Mental Health and Employee Counseling*. New York: Behavioral Publications, 1973.

Marshall, J. and C.L. Cooper, *The Mobile Manager and His Wife*. Bradford: MCB, 1976.

Office of Health Economics. *Off Sick*. Pamphlet No. 36. London, 1971.

Seidenberg, R., "Corporate Wives—Corporate Casualties," *American Management,* 1973.

Taylor, R., "Stress at Work," *New Society,* October 17, 1974.

CHAPTER 4

Benson, H., and others, "Decreased Systolic Blood Pressure in Hypertensive Subjects Who Practiced Meditation," *Journal of Clinical Investigation,* 52, 1973, 8.

Benson, H., and others, "Decreased Blood Pressure in Pharmacologically Treated Hypertensive Patients Who Regularly Elicited the Relaxation Response," *The Lancet,* February 1974, 289-91.

Blackwell, B., and others, "TM in Hypertension. Individual Response Patterns," *The Lancet,* 1, 1976, 223-26.

Bortner, R.W. and R.H. Rosenman, "The Measurement of Pattern A Behavior," *Journal of Chronic Diseases,* 20, 1967, 525-33.

Brown, B.B., *Stress and the Art of Biofeedback*. New York: Harper and Row, 1977.

Dillbeck, M.C., "The Effect of TM Technique on Anxiety Level," *Clinical Psychology,* 33 (4), 1977, 1076-78.

Friedman, M.D. and R.H. Rosenman, *Type A Behavior and Your Heart.* New York: Knopf, 1974.

Gavin, J.F., "Occupational Mental Health—Forces and Trends," *Personnel Journal,* 1977, 198-201.

Jacobson, E., *Progressive Relaxation.* Chicago: University of Chicago Press, 1958.

Kuna, D.J., "Meditation and Work," *Vocational Guidance Quarterly,* 23 (4), 1975, 342-46.

Marshall, J. and C.L. Cooper, *Executives Under Pressure.* London: Macmillan, 1979.

Michaels, R.R., and others, "Evaluation of TM as a Method of Reducing Stress," *Science,* 192, 1976, 1242-44.

Patel, C., "Twelve Month Follow-up of Yoga and Biofeedback in the Management of Hypertension," *The Lancet,* January 1975, 62-64.

Peters, R.K. and H. Benson, "Time Out From Tension," *Harvard Business Review,* January-February, 1979, 120-24.

Puryear, H.B., and others, "Anxiety Reduction Associated with Meditation: Home Study," *Perceptual and Motor Skills,* 43, 1976, 527-31.

Suinn, R.M., "How to Break the Vicious Cycle of Stress," *Psychology Today,* 1976, 59-60.

CHAPTER 5

Buck, V., *Working Under Pressure.* London: Staples Press, 1972.

Burke, R.J., J. Firth and C. McGratten, "Husband-Wife Compatibility and the Management of Stress," *Journal of Social Psychology,* 94, 1974, 243-52.

Caplan, G., "The Family as a Support System," in G. Caplan and M. Killilea (eds.) *Support Systems and Mutual Help.* New York: Grune and Stratton.

Caplan, R.D., S. Cobb, J.R.P. French, R. Van Harrison and S.R. Pinneau, "Job Demands and Worker Health: Main Effects and Occupational Differences," *NIOSH Research Report,* 1975.

Coch, L. and J.R.P. French, "Overcoming Resistance to Change," *Human Relations,* 1, 1948, 512-32.

Colligan, M.J. and L.R. Murphy, "Mass Psychogenic Illness in Organizations," *Journal of Occupational Psychology,* 52, 1979, 77-90.

Cooper, C.L. and J. Marshall, *Understanding Executive Stress*. London: Macmillan, 1978.

Cooper, C.L. and E. Mumford, *The Quality of Working Life in Western and Eastern Europe*. London: Associated Business Press, 1979.

Cooper, C.L. and R. Payne, *Stress at Work*. London: John Wiley & Sons, 1978.

Cooper, C.L. and R. Payne, *Current Concerns in Occupational Stress*. London: John Wiley & Sons, 1980.

Eitinger, L. and A. Strom, "Mortality and Morbidity after Excessive Stress: a Follow-up Investigation of Norwegian Concentration Camp Survivors," *Humanities*, 1973.

Fiedler, F.E., *A Theory of Leadership Effectiveness*. New York: McGraw-Hill, 1967.

French, J.R.P. and R.D. Caplan, "Organizational Stress and Individual Strain," in A.J. Marrow (ed.) *The Failure of Success*. New York: Amacom, 1973, pp. 30-66.

French, J.R.P., J. Israel and D. As, "An Experiment in Participation in a Norwegian Factory," *Human Relations*, 13 (1), 1960, 3-20.

Gore, S., "The Effect of Social Support in Moderating the Health Consequences of Unemployment," *Journal of Health and Social Behavior*, 19, 1978, 15-165.

La Rocco, J.M. and A.P. Jones, "Co-worker and Leader Support as Moderators of Stress-Strain Relationships in Work Situations," *Journal of Applied Psychology*, 63, 5, 1978, 629-34.

Luisada, A.A., "Introduction of Symposium on the Epidemiology of Heart Disease," *American Journal of Cardiology*, 10, 1962, 316.

Mansfield, R., "The Initiation of Graduates in Industry: The Resolution of Identity-Stress as a Determinant of Job Satisfaction in the Early Months at Work," *Human Relations*, 25, 1972, 77-86.

Margolis, B.L., W.H. Kroes and R.P. Quinn, "Job Stress: An Unlisted Occupational Hazard," *Journal of Occupational Medicine*, 16, 10, 1974, 654-61.

Marmot, M.G., and others, "Epidemiologic Studies of Coronary Heart Disease and Stroke in Japanese Men Living in Japan, Hawaii and California: Prevalence of Coronary and Hypertensive Heart Disease and Associated Risk Factors," *American Journal of Epidemiology*, 102, 6, 1975, 514-25.

Matsumoto, Y.S., "Social Stress and Coronary Heart Disease in Japan," *Milbank Memorial Fund Quarterly*, 48, 1970.

Morris, J., "Managerial Stress and 'the Cross of Relationships'," in D. Gowler and K. Legge (eds.) *Managerial Stress*. Epping: Gower Press, 1975.

Myers, J., J. Lindenthal and M. Pepper, "Life Events, Social Integration and Psychiatric Symptomatology," *Journal of Health and Social Behavior*, 16, 1975, 121-27.

Payne, R., "Organizational Stress and Social Support," in C.L. Cooper and R. Payne (eds.) *Current Concerns in Occupational Stress*. London: John Wiley & Sons, 1980.

Peters, R.K. and H. Benson, "Time Out From Tension," *Harvard Business Review*, January-February, 1979, 120-24.

Smith, M.J., M.J. Colligan and J.J. Hurrell, "Three Incidents of Industrial Psychogenic Illness," *Journal of Occupational Medicine*, 20, 6, 1978, 401-2.

Wilson, E.O., *Sociobiology*. Cambridge, Mass.: Harvard University Press, 1975.

CHAPTER 6

Albrecht, K., *Stress and the Manager: Making It Work For You*. Englewood Cliffs, New Jersey: Prentice-Hall, 1979.

Bass, B.M., "Exercise Future," *A Program of Exercises for Management and Organizational Psychology*. Rochester: The University of Rochester, 1970.

Brown, G.W., F. Sklair, T.O. Harris and J.L.T. Birley, "Life Events and Psychiatric Disorders, Part I: Some Methodological Issues," *Psychological Medicine*, 3, (1), 1973.

Dyer, W.W., *Your Erroneous Zones*. New York: Avon Books, 1976.

Heller, J., *Something Happened*. New York: Ballantine Books, 1975.

Holmes, T.H. and M. Masuda, "Life Change and Illness Susceptibility," *Separation and Depression* AAAS, 1973, 161-86.

Mechanic, D., "Discussion of Studies Relating Changes and Illness," in B.S. Dohrenwald and B.P. Dohrenwald (eds.) *Stressful Life Events: Their Nature and Effects*. New York: Wiley, 1974, pp. 87-98.

Myers, J., J. Lindenthal and M. Pepper, "Life Events, Social Integration and Psychiatric Symptomatology," *Journal of Health and Social Behavior,* 16, 1975, 121-27.

Pfeiffer, J.W. and J.E. Jones, *Structured Experiences for Human Relations Training.* Iowa City: University Associates Press, 1970.

Steinmetz, J., "The Stress Reduction Program at University Hospital University of California Medical Center, San Diego," *NIOSH Conference on Occupational Stress,* November, 1977.

Wyler, A.R., T.H. Holmes and M. Masuda, "Magnitude of Life Events and Seriousness of Illness," *Psychosomatic Medicine,* 33, 1971, 115-22.

CHAPTER 7

Bailyn, L., "Career and Family Orientations of Husbands and Wives in Relation to Marital Happiness," *Human Relations,* 23, 1970, 97-113.

Cooper, C.L. and J. Marshall, *Understanding Executive Stress.* London: Macmillan, 1978.

Farid, S.M., *The Current Tempo of Fertility in England and Wales.* London: HMSO, 1974.

Fogarty, M.P., R. Rapoport and R.N. Rapoport, *Sex, Career and Family.* Beverly Hills: Sage, 1971.

Foster, L.W., J.C. Latack and L.J. Riendl, "Effects and Promises of the Shortened Work Week," *Proceedings of the Academy of Management,* August, 1979.

Fried, M., "Transitional Functions of Working Class Communities: Implications for Forced Relocation," in M.B. Kantor (ed.) *Mobility and Mental Health,* Conference on Community Mental Health Research, Fifth Washington University Social Science Institute Conference. St. Louis: Thomas, 1965.

Glaser, B.G. and A.L. Strauss, *Status Passage.* London: Aldine, 1969.

Hall, F.S. and D.T. Hall, *The Two-Career Couple.* Reading, Mass.: Addison-Wesley, 1979.

Hall, D.T. and F.S. Hall, "Stress and the Two Career Couple," in C.L. Cooper and R. Payne (eds.) *Current Concerns in Occupational Stress.* London: John Wiley & Sons, 1980, pp. 243-65.

Handy, C., "The Family: Help or Hindrance?," in C.L. Cooper and R.

Payne (eds.) *Stress At Work.* London: John Wiley & Sons, 1978, pp. 107–23.

Marshall, J. and Cooper, C.L., *The Mobile Manager and His Wife.* Bradford: MCB, 1976.

Packard, V., *A Nation of Strangers.* New York: McKay, 1972.

Pahl, J.M. and R.E. Pahl, *Managers and Their Wives.* London: Allen Lane, 1971.

Rapoport, R. and R.N. Rapoport, *Dual Career Families Re-Examined.* London: Martin Robertson, 1976.

Renshaw, J.R., "He Can't Even Manage His Own Family," *Wharton Magazine,* Winter 1977, 42–47.

Seidenberg, R., *Corporate Wives—Corporate Casualties.* New York: American Management Association, 1973.

Staines, G.L., J.H. Pleck, L. Shepard and P. O'Connor, "Wives' Employment Status and Marital Adjustment," unpublished manuscript, Institute for Social Research, University of Michigan, 1979.

CHAPTER 8

Beveridge, W.E., *The Interview in Staff Appraisal.* London: Allen and Unwin, 1974.

Birch, S. and B. Macmillan, *Managers on the Move: A Study of British Managerial Mobility.* London: B.I.M. Report No. 7, 1970.

British Institute of Management. *Executive Health Care.* London: B.I.M., 1971.

Campbell, J., E.E. Lawler, M. Dunnette and K.E. Weick, *Managerial Behavior, Performance and Effectiveness.* New York: McGraw-Hill, 1970.

Cooper, C.L., *Theories of Group Processes.* London: John Wiley & Sons, 1975.

Cooper, C.L., *Learning From Others in Groups.* London: Associated Business Press, 1979.

Cooper, C.L. and J. Marshall, *Understanding Executive Stress.* London: Macmillan, 1978.

Cooper, C.L. and R. Payne, *Current Concerns in Occupational Stress.* London: John Wiley & Sons, 1980.

Glueck, W.F., *Personnel: A Diagnostic Approach.* Homewood, Illinois: Irwin-Dorsey, 1974.

Hackman, J.R. and E.E. Lawler, "Employee Reactions to Job Characteristics," *Journal of Applied Psychology,* 55, 1971.

Lazarus, R.S., "Cognitive and Personality Factors Underlying Threat and Coping," in M.H. Appley and R. Trumbull (eds.) *Psychological Stress.* New York: Appleton, 1967.

Marshall, J. and C.L. Cooper, *The Mobile Manager and His Wife.* Bradford: MCB, 1976.

Page, N., "Executive Unemployment and Personal Redundancy," *Personnel Review,* 5, 2, 1976.

Prentice, G., "Faith at Work: The Message is the Mission," *Personnel Management,* 8, 3, 1976.

Randell, G.A., and others, *Staff Appraisal.* London: Institute of Personnel Management, 1972.

Roethlisberger, F.J. and W.J. Dickson, *Management and the Worker.* Cambridge, Mass.: Harvard University Press, 1939.

Stewart, R., *Contrasts in Management.* New York: McGraw-Hill, 1976.

Weir, D., "Radical Managerialism: Middle Managers' Perceptions of Collective Bargaining," *British Journal of Industrial Relations,* XIV, 3, 1976.

CHAPTER 9

Bennis, W.G. and P.E. Slater, *The Temporary Society.* New York: Harper and Row, 1968.

Burns, T. and G.M. Stalker, *The Management of Innovation.* London: Tavistock, 1961.

Cooper, C.L., *The Executive Gypsy: The Quality of Managerial Life.* London: Macmillan, 1979.

Cooper, C.L. and J. Marshall, *Understanding Executive Stress.* London: Macmillan, 1978.

Golembiewski, B.T. and M. McConkie, "The Centrality of Interpersonal Trust," in C.L. Cooper (ed.) *Theories of Group Processes.* London: John Wiley & Sons, 1975.

Harrison, R., "Role Negotiation: A Tough-Minded Approach to Team

Development," in M.L. Berger and P.J. Berger (eds.) *Group Training Techniques*. Epping: Gower Press, 1972, pp. 83-97.

Jones, J.E. and J.J. Jones, "Dialog: A Program for Developing Work Relationships," in J.W. Pfeiffer and J.E. Jones (eds.) *Structured Experiences for Human Relations Training*. San Diego: University Associates, 1973.

Lazarus, R.S., "Cognitive and Personality Factors Underlying Threat and Coping," in M.H. Appley and R. Trumbull (eds.) *Psychological Stress*. New York: Appleton, 1967.

Mellinger, G.D., "Interpersonal Trust as a Factor in Communication," *Journal of Abnormal and Social Psychology*, 52, 1956, 304-9.

Rogers, C., *Encounter Groups*. London: Allen Lane, 1970.

Wright, H.B., *Executive Ease and Dis-ease*. Epping: Gower Press, 1975.

Index